S0-APN-045

Bilingual/Bicultural Program
C. K. McClatchy High School

Launch into Reading

THOMSON

HEINLE

Australia   Canada   Mexico   Singapore   Spain   United Kingdom   United States

THOMSON

HEINLE

Launch into Reading Student Book

Vice President, Editorial Director ESL: *Nancy Leonhardt*
Director of School Publishing: *Edward Lamprich*
Managing Developmental Editor: *Donna Schaffer*
Associate Developmental Editor: *Tania Maundrell-Brown*
Senior Production Editor: *Michael Burggren*
Manufacturing Manager: *Marcia Locke*
Director of Global ESL Training and Development: *Evelyn Nelson*
Marketing Manager: *Jim McDonough*
Editorial Assistant: *Elizabeth Allen*
Development, Design, and Production: *The GTS Companies*
Cover Illustrator: *David Diaz*
Cover Photograph (Alcatraz): *Richard T. Nowitz/CORBIS*
Printer: *R.R. Donnelley and Sons Company, Willard*

Printed in the United States of America
3 4 5 6 7 8 9 10 06 05 04 03 02

ISBN: 0-8384-0122-8

For more information contact Heinle, 25 Thomson Place, Boston, Massachusetts 02210 USA,
or you can visit our Internet site at http://www.heinle.com

Dear Student

Welcome to *Launch into Reading*! There are three levels in this program. Each one will help you to read, write, listen, and speak effectively. Your textbook is divided into four units. There are four reading selections in each unit. The reading selections are related to each other by theme.

The readings in each unit are both fiction and nonfiction. Many well-known authors wrote these selections. Some of the readings are traditional and classic. Some of them are contemporary. We hope you enjoy reading them. At the end of each unit, you will find suggestions for other books to read.

There are helpful activities and strategies that go along with each reading. Before you read each selection, you will think about your own background and what you already know, then learn some new vocabulary words and find out how to use a reading strategy. As you read, you will get a chance to use the reading strategy. Your teacher will help you learn more about how to spell and sound out words. After you finish the reading, you will get a chance to show what you learned. You will connect what you learned to other classes that you are taking and to real life. You will also learn more about words, grammar, and writing.

As you use *Launch into Reading*, you will have a lot of support. Your *Student Workbook* and the *Student CD-ROM* will give you extra practice. At the end of each unit, you will be able to use everything you learned when you do the unit project. The projects are fun and will give you a chance to work with other students and use English outside of the classroom. You will also have a chance to work on the Internet.

We hope you have fun as you learn English with *Launch into Reading*. A whole world of possibilities awaits you!

Acknowledgments

Reviewers and Consultants

We want to thank our reviewers and consultants who made valuable contributions to *Launch into Reading.* The reviewers and consultants evaluated selections and provided advice on current pedagogy.

Consulting Author
Florence Decker has taught ESL in El Paso ISD and Dallas ISD, Texas. She has also conducted ESL methodology classes at the University of Texas in El Paso and at Centro de Lenguas in Juarez, Mexico. In addition, she has been involved in writing curricula for several school districts.

- **Donna Altes**
  Silverado Middle School
  Napa, California

- **Cally Andriotis-Williams**
  Newcomers High School
  Long Island City, New York

- **Lynn Clausen**
  Pajaro Valley Unified
  School District
  Watsonville, California

- **Mary Hadley**
  Georgia Southern University
  Statesboro, Georgia

- **Erik Johansen**
  Hueneme High School
  Oxnard, California

- **Cherylyn Smith**
  Fresno Unified School District
  Fresno, California

Contents

Launch into Reading

UNIT 1
Friendship

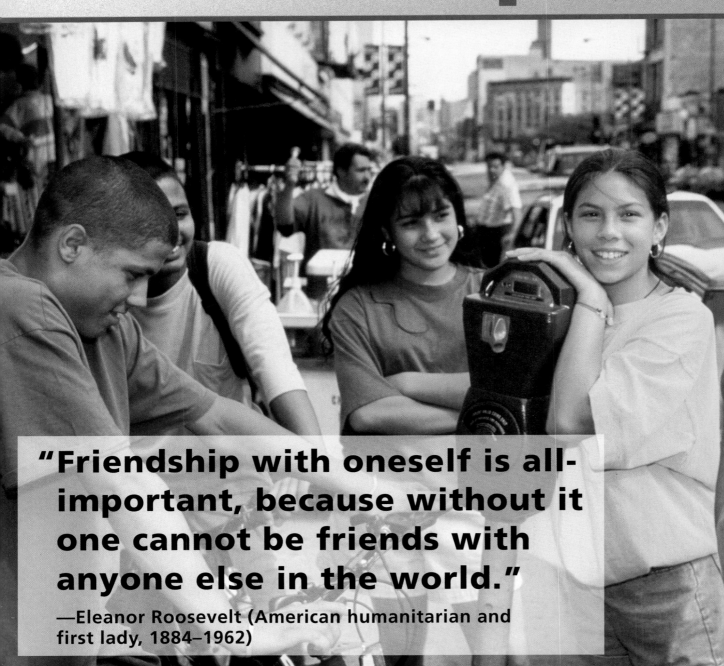

"Friendship with oneself is all-important, because without it one cannot be friends with anyone else in the world."

—Eleanor Roosevelt (American humanitarian and first lady, 1884–1962)

Discuss the Theme
Making Friends

A friend can be a classmate, a relative, or anyone with whom you enjoy spending your time or sharing your thoughts and feelings. Sometimes all you need to begin a friendship is a smile or a kind look as in "Friendly in a Friendly Way." Occasionally, friendships can develop from negative experiences, such as in "Yang's First Friend." You'll see that a friend does not always have to be a person, as in the excerpt of "The Fox" from the story *The Little Prince.* In "Greg and Willie," friendship develops from need and companionship. Think of your own friends as you read about these unusual and interesting friendships.

- Do you think you are a friendly person?
- How did you make your first friend at school?
- Has a good friend of yours ever moved away? How did you feel?
- What are some of the ways that true friends help each other?

WRITING FOCUS:
Fictional Narrative

Before You Read

Background

How do you feel on a sunny day? In the following poem, the poet feels so happy that he wants to say "Hello" to everyone and everything he sees. In this poem, you'll read about how one person expresses friendly feelings in a light-hearted way.

Friendly in a Friendly Way

**a poem by
Langston Hughes**

LEARNING OBJECTIVES

- Identify and analyze recurring themes across works
- Identify nouns and verbs as parts of speech
- Identify repeated words in poetry
- Identify point of view

Building Your Vocabulary

1. With a partner, read the words at the bottom of the page. They are all different ways of moving your head. Discuss the meanings of these words. Try moving your head in different ways and see if your partner can guess which words describe what you are doing.

nod   shake   tilt   hang   roll

Reading: Clarify word meanings through example

2. The words below describe facial expressions. Discuss them with your partner. Use a dictionary if you don't know the meaning. Try showing your partner each of these expressions. Talk about what makes you smile, grin, stare, grimace, or frown. On a separate sheet of paper, write a sentence using each word.

smile   grin   stare   grimace   frown

Reading Strategy

Identify themes   The *theme* is the central message or idea of a poem or story. When you identify the theme, ask yourself: What is this poem (or story) really about? What central message is it trying to communicate? Common themes that appear in poems and stories include loyalty, friendship, family, and courage.

The poet Langston Hughes.

Applying the Reading Strategy

1. Titles can often give important clues to what the author is trying to communicate. Take a close look at the title.

2. Read the poem carefully to get an impression of what it's about. Read the poem a second time and ask yourself: "What is the poem trying to say?"

3. To identify the theme, think about important ideas, such as honesty, love, loyalty, and friendship. What theme is the poet trying to communicate here?

4. What similarities and differences do you notice between the theme in this poem and the theme in other poems and stories you have read?

Reading: Identify and analyze recurring themes across works

Friendly in a Friendly Way

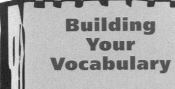
As You Read

1. Look at the title of this poem. What does it tell you about the theme?

2. How does the poem make you feel?

3. Reread the last stanza. What do you think the poet is trying to say?

A poem by Langston Hughes

I nodded at the sun
And the sun said, *Howdy do!*
I nodded at the tree
And the tree said, *Howdy, too!*

I shook hands with the bush.
The bush shook hands with me.
I said to the flower,
Flower, how do you be?

I spoke to the man.
The strange man touched his hat.
I smiled at the woman—
The world is smiling yet.

Oh, it's a holiday
When everybody feels that way!
What way?—*Friendly*
In a friendly way.

Howdy do!: Hello!
strange: unfamiliar

Science

What happens when the sun and green plants meet each other? *Photosynthesis!* Green plants turn energy from the sun into chemical energy through the process of photosynthesis. A green substance called **chlorophyll,** found in the leaves of plants, gets energy from the sun.

About the Author

Langston Hughes (1902–1967)

Langston Hughes was born in Joplin, Missouri. He wrote novels, plays, and hundreds of poems that deal with the life and experiences of African Americans. He used the rhythms of blues and jazz, as well as the language of Harlem in his poetry. Langston Hughes continued to write and lecture until his death in 1967.

Reading: Identify and analyze recurring themes across works

After You Read

Retell It!

Work in small groups. List the ways the narrator acted in a friendly way. Put them together in order. Take turns reading them aloud.

Think, Discuss, Write

Discuss these questions in small groups. Write your answers.

1. **Recall details**   Who or what does the poet communicate with in the poem?

2. **Tone**   Do you think the poet is happy? Give examples of the images used to show this.

3. **Compare and contrast**   You can recognize a poem by the way it looks on the page. How does "Friendly in a Friendly Way" look different from a paragraph in one of your textbooks?

4. **Recall details**   What does the poet greet first?

5. **Make inferences**   Do you think the poet actually shakes hands with a bush? Why or why not?

6. **Cause and effect**   Why do you think the poet says "it's a holiday" when people feel "that way"?

7. **Make inferences**   Why do you think the narrator touches his hat?

Reading: Retell the central ideas of simple narrative passages

What's Your Opinion?

Work in a small group. Discuss what you did or did not like about the poem "Friendly in a Friendly Way." Divide a sheet of paper into two columns. At the top of one write *Liked because* and at the top of the other write *Disliked because*. Write down your reasons for liking or disliking the poem. Choose one person in your group to present your opinions to the class.

Launch into Grammar

Nouns and verbs   Each word in the English language can be identified as a part of speech. Two of the most important parts of speech are nouns and verbs. **Nouns** are words that name a person, place, or thing. Examples of nouns include: *girl, forest,* and *rock.* There are two types of **verbs.** Verbs that show **action** include: *run, think, bring,* and *throw.* Verbs of **being** are words that say something "exists," such as: *am, be, were,* and *become.*

Find the nouns and verbs in each sentence. List each noun and verb on a separate sheet of paper.

1. I nodded at the sun.

2. I shook hands with the bush.

3. The strange man touched his hat.

 For more practice with parts of speech, complete page 3 of the Student Workbook.

Written Conventions: Identify all parts of speech

Launch into Word Analysis

Word repetition In poetry, words, sounds, images, and ideas are often repeated. This repetition can show a different meaning of the word. For example, the repetition of the word *friendly* in the poem helps make its meaning clear. What does the phrase "friendly in a friendly way" mean to you?

Read this poem with a partner.

"The Magic Touch"
Touch is a touchy word
That can touch you in many ways
Touching can be touching
If you've got the touch, it pays.
So keep in touch, be in touch
For now and the rest of your days.

How many different meanings can you find for the word *touch*? On a separate sheet of paper, make a list of the meanings. Use your dictionary to help you.

Extend: Add unfamiliar words from your reading of magazines, newspapers, or textbooks to your Vocabulary Log. Use context clues to help you figure out their meanings.

 For more practice with word repetition, complete page 4 of the Student Workbook.

Reading: Identify and interpret figurative language and words with multiple meanings

Launch into Writing

Point of view The outlook and attitude that a writer has toward a subject is called a **point of view.** More than one point of view can be used for a poem or story. A writer can describe or view the action from the inside or the outside. The "inside" point of view is called the first-person voice (I, me, we, us). The "outside" point of view is called the third-person voice (he, she, they, them).

When you write, choose a point of view that you are comfortable with and fits what you're writing about. Once you decide on a point of view, use it for the entire poem or story. The first verse of the poem *Friendly in a Friendly Way* is written from a first-person ("I") point of view. With a partner, try re-writing the verse from a third-person point of view. An example is shown for you.

First-person point of view	Third-person point of view
I nodded at the sun	Langston nodded at the sun
I nodded at the tree	Langston nodded at the tree

Write two verses of the poem with a third-person voice. Then try writing your own short poem using either a first-person or third-person point of view.

 For more practice with point of view, complete pages 6–7 of the Student Workbook.

Writing: Select a focus, an organizational structure, and a point of view based on purpose, audience, length, and format requirements

2

Before You Read

Yang's First Friend

an excerpt from a novel
by Lensey Namioka

Background

Have you ever had to change schools? If you have, then you know how hard it can be. In this excerpt from "Yang's First Friend," you will see how one boy learns to adjust to his new North American school and how he makes his first American friend.

LEARNING OBJECTIVES

- Identify point of view in literature
- Identify descriptive words: adjectives and adverbs
- Identify idioms, metaphors, and similes in prose
- Develop a point of view

Building Your Vocabulary

Idioms are expressions that do not mean the same as the individual words. For example, the literal meaning of "hit the roof" is "hit the top of the house." The figurative meaning is "become angry."

Discuss the following idioms with a partner. Make a chart on a separate sheet of paper and write down what you think the idioms on page 13 mean. As you read the story, see if your guesses were correct.

Reading: Identify idioms in prose; Reading: Understand and explain the figurative and metaphorical use of words in context

Idiom	Meaning
keep each other company (p. 14)	*spend time with someone so each of you doesn't feel alone*

What do these idioms mean? Add them to your chart.

1. have no trouble at all (p. 15)

2. hold something against someone (p. 15)

3. spend time with someone (p. 16)

Reading Strategy

Recognize point of view   When you read a story, pay attention to the point of view from which it is told. Does the storyteller use words like **I** and **we** or words like **he, she,** and **they**? Does the story tell you what all the characters are thinking, or just how one particular character feels?

Applying the Reading Strategy

As you read "Yang's First Friend," ask yourself these questions:

1. Who is telling the story?

2. Is the story told from an *omniscient* point of view? This means the person telling the story knows everything about every character.

3. Is the story told from the *first-person* point of view? This means a character in the story tells the story, using the word **I**.

4. Is the narrator reliable? Are the facts presented objectively or is the person telling the story biased?

5. What is the overall theme of the story? How does the point of view affect the story's theme?

Reading: Contrast points of view in narrative text and explain how they affect the overall theme of the work

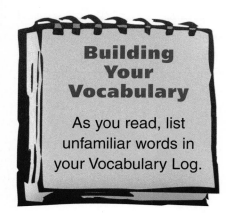

Building Your Vocabulary

As you read, list unfamiliar words in your Vocabulary Log.

As You Read

1. Who is telling this story?

2. Why do American kids laugh at the narrator?

3. Does the narrator know what everyone else is thinking?

Yang's First Friend

an excerpt from a novel by Lensey Namioka

Before I got used to the American school, the other kids laughed at some of the things I did. Each morning, as soon as the teacher came into the room, I jumped to my feet and stood stiffly at attention. That was how we showed our respect to the teacher in China.

The first time I did it here, the teacher asked me whether I needed something. I looked around and saw that nobody else was standing up. Feeling foolish, I shook my head and sat down.

When I did it again the next day, a couple of kids behind me started to snigger. After that, I remembered not to jump up, but I half rose a few times. One boy used to watch me, and if he saw my bottom leave my seat, he would whisper, "Down, Fido!"

Third Sister was a great help during those early days. While the other kids were busy talking or playing games at recess, she and I stood in a corner and kept each other company.

Every day we walked together to our elementary school, which was not far from our house. Eldest Brother and Second Sister took a big yellow bus to a school that was farther away.

If Eldest Brother had trouble making friends, it didn't seem to bother him. Music was the only thing he really cared about.

snigger: laugh in a sly or sneaky way

14 **UNIT 1** **Friendship**

Reading: Contrast points of view in narrative text and explain how they affect the overall theme of the work

I think Second Sister felt the loneliest. In China, people always said she would turn out to be a real beauty. She had been popular at school there, always surrounded by friends. But in America not many people told her she was beautiful. These days she was often cranky and sad. Mother told the rest of us that we just had to be patient with Second Sister.

Third Sister had no trouble at all making friends. Even before she could speak much English, she began chatting with other kids. She could always fill in the gaps with laughter.

During lunch she and I sat at a table with mostly Asian-Americans. At first we didn't understand what Asian-Americans were. When we were filling out registration forms at school, we put down "Chinese" in the space marked "race."

The secretary at the school told us to change it to "Asian-American." With a big smile, she said, "We have a number of Asian-Americans at this school, so you'll be able to make friends easily."

My teacher must have felt the same because on my first day in class, she seated me next to a girl who was also Asian-American.

I greeted her in Chinese, but she just shook her head. "I'm afraid I don't understand Japanese," she said in English.

"I wasn't speaking Japanese," I told her. "I was speaking Chinese."

"Sorry. I don't understand that, either. My family is from Korea."

I didn't know much about Korea, except that my country had once invaded her country. I hoped she didn't hold it against me.

Reading: Contrast points of view in narrative text and explain how they affect the overall theme of the work

"You speak good English," I said. "When did you arrive?"

"I was born in America," she said. "So were my parents."

In spite of this bad start, she tried to be helpful to me. But we never became close friends.

So I was lonely. After Third Sister made friends in her class, she began to spend less and less time with me.

Then I met Matthew. During recess one day, Third Sister was busy talking to some new friends, and I was looking wistfully at some boys playing catch and wondering if I could find the nerve to join them.

Suddenly I felt someone pluck my pen from my pocket. This was a ballpoint pen I had brought with me from China, with a picture of a panda on the side of it. Whenever I thought about China and missed the friends I had left behind, I would take out the pen and look at the picture.

The boy who had taken the pen was running away, laughing. I ran after him, shouting. The teacher came up and asked me what the trouble was.

"He took my ... my ..." I stopped, because I didn't know the English word for pen. In Chinese we have the same word, *bi,* for pen, pencil, and brush. "He took my writing stick," I finished lamely.

The boy who'd taken the pen stood there and grinned, while the teacher looked puzzled.

wistfully: sadly
lamely: weakly

Reading: Contrast points of view in narrative text and explain how they affect the overall theme of the work

"Jake took his ballpoint pen," said a tall, freckled boy with curly brown hair. "I saw the whole thing."

The teacher turned and frowned at Jake. "Is this true?"

"Aw, I was just teasing him a little," said Jake, quickly handing the pen back to me. "He's always playing with it, so I got curious."

I thanked the boy with the curly hair. "Don't mind Jake," he said. "He didn't mean anything."

"My name is Yang Yingtao," I introduced myself. Then I remembered that in America people said their family name last and their given name first.

"Yingtao is my last name," I told him. "Except that in America my last name is really my first name and my first name is my last name. So I'm Yang Yingtao in China and Yingtao Yang in America."

The boy looked confused. Just then the bell rang. "I'm Matthew Conner," he said quickly. "See you around!"

I began to feel a little less lonely.

As You Read

1. How does Matthew help Yang?

2. How are Matthew and Jake alike to Yang? How are they different?

3. What makes Yang feel less lonely?

About the Author
Lensey Namioka (b. 1929)

Lensey Namioka was born in Beijing, China. She moved to the United States with her family, where she attended Radcliffe College and the University of California, Berkeley. Her family name is Chao. Lensey Namioka has written books for children and adults. Two of her books were selected as Best Book of the Year by the American Library Association.

Reading: Contrast points of view in narrative text and explain how they affect the overall theme of the work

After You Read

Retell It!

How do you think Matthew Connor felt about the pen incident? Rewrite the story from his point of view.

Think, Discuss, Write

Discuss these questions in small groups. Then write your answers on a separate sheet of paper.

1. **Compare and contrast**   How did Yang greet his teacher in China? How did the class greet his teacher at the American school?

2. **Recall details**   Who keeps Yang company at school?

3. **Recall details**   Explain why Yang feels lonely at his new school.

4. **Recall details**   What did it take to help Yang start to feel less lonely at his new school?

5. **Cause and effect**   Is there a way you could help students in your school feel less lonely and more involved?

6. **Make predictions**   What do you think will happen next in the story?

7. **Comprehension**   Would a gesture such as Matthew's help you feel less lonely if you were Yang?

What's Your Opinion?

Do you think that Yang is a reliable narrator? Do you believe the things he says about how other people

Reading: Make reasonable assertions about a text through accurate, supporting citations feel? Working with a small group, take turns being Eldest Brother, Second Sister, and Third Sister. Describe your feelings about your new school.

Launch into Grammar

Descriptive words **Adjectives** and **adverbs** are descriptive words.

Adjectives describe or give information about nouns and pronouns. They tell you

- what kind (*blue, happy, scary*)
- which one (*this, that*)
- how many (*three, twenty-five, many*)

Adverbs tell you something about a verb or another adverb. They tell you

- where (*here, there, inside*)
- when (*now, then, soon, yesterday*)
- how (*slowly, anxiously, happily*)
- how often or how long (*never, sometimes, twice*)
- how much (*extremely, too, more*)

On a piece of paper, write down the following sentences. Then, with a partner, underline the adjectives and circle the adverbs.

1. Every day we walked to the elementary school.

2. I quickly jumped to my feet and stood stiffly.

3. I then thanked the boy with the curly hair.

 For more practice with descriptive words, use page 11 of the Student Workbook.

Written Conventions: Use adjectives correctly in writing and speaking; Written Conventions: Use adverbs correctly in writing and speaking

Launch into Word Analysis

Metaphors and similes   A *metaphor* compares two things directly. A *simile* compares two things using either *like* or *as*. Both help you see a familiar object in a new way.

Simile: In the middle of the pool, other swimmers were splashing around *like sharks*.

Metaphor: The other swimmers were *sharks*, splashing around in the pool.

What two things are being compared? How does comparison help you imagine how the speaker might feel about learning to swim?

Work with a partner. Write three sentences that contain similes and three that contain metaphors. Share your sentences with the rest of the class.

> **Extend:** Form creative comparisons as you study material in other classes. For instance, a historical figure famous for being clever might remind you of a fox.

Study Tip

Find a quiet place where you can do your homework and your writing. Make this your "study place."

For more practice using metaphors and similes, complete page 12 of the Student Workbook.

Reading: Identify metaphors and similes in prose

Launch into Writing

Develop a point of view *Yang's First Friend* is a fictional piece written from the first-person point of view. When Yang tells his story, he uses words such as **I, me,** and **we;** this shows the reader that the story contains Yang's opinions and is written from his own **point of view.**

Retell a story about a moment in your life and how that moment or event is special to you. When you finish, exchange papers with a friend. Have your friend make a plot diagram for your story and identify your point of view.

Students complete a writing assignment.

Last Summer

Last summer, my family visited Aunt Judy at her cabin near the lake. When we got there, my sister Liz and I played outside until supper.

After supper, my mom said that it was too dark to play outside. We were mad. Aunt Judy does not have a television set and we couldn't find anything to do.

Then, Judy's friend Joan came over. She brought her guitar. We all sang songs until after midnight. It was lots of fun.

For more practice with developing a point of view, use pages 14–15 of the Student Workbook.

Writing: Select a focus, an organizational structure, and a point of view based upon purpose, audience, length, and format requirements

3

Background

The Little Prince is a fictional story about the adventures of a boy from another planet. In this selection called "The Fox," the little prince has a conversation with a fox. The fox helps him learn about the meaning of friendship.

The Fox

an excerpt from a novel by Antoine de Saint-Exupéry

LEARNING OBJECTIVES

- Identify character traits
- Recognize prepositions
- Learn to recognize multiple meanings of certain words
- Write a character sketch

Building Your Vocabulary

1. The story of "The Fox" involves many words that convey feelings or emotions. Read the list of words below. As you come upon them in the story, discuss them with a partner.

unhappy
happy
perplexed
bored
patient
worrying
embarrassed
responsible

2. With your partner, make a chart on a separate sheet of paper. Write down each word. Then give examples of some situations in which you might have these feelings.

Feeling	Situation
Unhappy	*When my best friend moved away*

Reading Strategy

Recognize character traits   Meeting a character in a story is a lot like meeting a real person. At first, you may not know quite what to make of the character. Slowly, story characters reveal who they are through what they do, say, and think. Sometimes, characters can confuse you. But usually, a clear picture of characters begins to appear as you keep reading.

Applying the Reading Strategy

1. Read descriptions of how a character looks. Try to picture the character in your mind. Is this character tall or short, old or young? Refer to the image you created whenever the character plays a role in the story.

2. Pay close attention to what the character says in the story's dialogue. What do the character's words reveal about that person?

3. In stories, as in real life, actions often speak louder than words. Carefully observe the character's behavior. Look for small clues at first. Then begin to put together a profile of the character. Is this character a likable person? Is he or she shy or outgoing? Is this someone you would trust?

4. As you read, let your knowledge of the characters help guide you through the story. Keep in mind that your view of a character could change as the events in the story change.

Reading: Analyze characterization as delineated through a character's thoughts, words, speech patterns, and actions, the narrator's description, and the thoughts, words, and actions of other characters

THE FOX

an excerpt from a novel by Antoine de Saint-Exupéry

It was then that the fox appeared.

"Good morning," said the fox.

"Good morning," the little prince responded politely, although when he turned around he saw nothing.

"I am right here," the voice said, "under the apple tree."

"Who are you?" asked the little prince, and added, "You are very pretty to look at."

"I am a fox," the fox said.

"Come and play with me," proposed the little prince. "I am so unhappy."

"I cannot play with you," the fox said. "I am not tamed ."

proposed: offered

tamed: under control and obedient

neglected: forgotten or disregarded

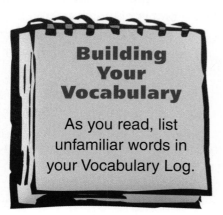

Building Your Vocabulary

As you read, list unfamiliar words in your Vocabulary Log.

"Ah! Please excuse me," said the little prince.

But, after some thought, he added:

"What does that mean—'tame'?"

"You do not live here," said the fox. "What is it that you are looking for?"

"I am looking for men," said the little prince. "What does that mean—'tame'?"

"Men," said the fox. "They have guns, and they hunt. It is very disturbing. They also raise chickens. These are their only interests. Are you looking for chickens?"

"No," said the little prince. "I am looking for friends. What does that mean—'tame'?"

"It is an act too often neglected ," said the fox. "It means to establish ties."

"'To establish ties'?"

"Just that," said the fox. "To me, you are still nothing more than a little boy who is just like a hundred thousand other little boys. And I have no need of you. And you, on your part, have no need of me. To you, I am nothing more than a fox like a hundred thousand other foxes. But if you tame me, then we shall need each

Reading: Analyze characterization as delineated through a character's thoughts, words, speech patterns, and actions, the narrator's description, and the thoughts, words, and actions of other characters

other. To me, you will be unique in all the world. To you, I shall be unique in all the world. . ."

"I am beginning to understand," said the little prince. "There is a flower . . . I think that she has tamed me."

"It is possible," said the fox. "On the Earth one sees all sorts of things."

"Oh, but this is not on the Earth!" said the little prince.

The fox seemed perplexed, and very curious.

"On another planet?"

"Yes."

"Are there hunters on that planet?"

"No."

"Ah, that is interesting! Are there chickens?"

"No."

unique: not like anything else; original
perplexed: unsure or confused

As You Read

1. Has the little prince ever seen a fox before? How do you know?

2. Is the little prince happy or sad when he meets the fox? Why?

3. What does the fox think about men?

4. What does the fox like and dislike about the little prince's planet? Why?

The Fox   25

Reading: Analyze characterization as delineated through a character's thoughts, words, speech patterns, and actions, the narrator's description, and the thoughts, words, and actions of other characters

"Nothing is perfect," sighed the fox. But he came back to his idea. "My life is very monotonous," he said. "I hunt chickens; men hunt me. All the chickens are just alike, and all the men are just alike. And, in consequence, I am a little bored. But if you tame me, it will be as if the sun came to shine on my life. I shall know the sound of a step that will be different from all the others. Other steps send me hurrying back underneath the ground. Yours will call me, like music, out of my burrow. And then look: you see the grain-fields down yonder? I do not eat bread. Wheat is of no use to me.

monotonous: boring and without change
burrow: a hole dug underground by animals for a home

The wheat fields have nothing to say to me. And that is sad. But you have hair that is the color of gold. Think how wonderful that will be when you have tamed me! The grain, which is also golden, will bring me back the thought of you. And I shall love to listen to the wind in the wheat. . ."

The fox gazed at the little prince, for a long time.

"Please—tame me!" he said.

"I want to, very much," the little prince replied. "But I have not much time. I have friends to discover, and a great many things to understand."

"One only understands the things that one tames," said the fox. "Men have no more time to understand anything. They buy things already made at the shops. But there is no shop anywhere where one can buy friendship, and so men have no friends anymore. If you want a friend, tame me. . ."

"What must I do, to tame you?" asked the little prince.

"You must be very patient," replied the fox. "First you will sit down at a little distance from me—like that—in the grass. I shall look at you out of the corner of my eye, and you will say nothing. Words are the source of

As You Read

1. What does the fox want the little prince to do? Why?
2. How does the fox define a *rite*?

Reading: Analyze characterization as delineated through a character's thoughts, words, speech patterns, and actions, the narrator's description, and the thoughts, words, and actions of other characters

misunderstandings. But you will sit a little closer to me, every day. . ."

The next day the little prince came back.

"It would have been better to come back at the same hour," said the fox. "If, for example, you came at four o'clock in the afternoon, then at three o'clock I shall begin to be happy. I shall feel happier and happier as the hour advances. At four o'clock, I shall already be worrying and jumping about. I shall show you how happy I am! But if you come at just any time, I shall never know at what hour my heart is to be ready to greet you. . . . One must observe the proper rites. . ."

"What is a rite?" asked the little prince.

"Those also are actions too often neglected," said the fox. "They are what make one day different from other days, one hour from other hours. There is a rite, for example, among my hunters. Every Thursday they dance with the village girls. So Thursday is a wonderful day for me! I can take a walk as far as the vineyards. But if the hunters danced at just any time, every day would be like every other day, and I should never have any vacation at all."

So the little prince tamed the fox. And when the hour of his departure drew near—

"Ah," said the fox, "I shall cry."

Reading: Analyze characterization as delineated through a character's thoughts, words, speech patterns, and actions, the narrator's description, and the thoughts, words, and actions of other characters

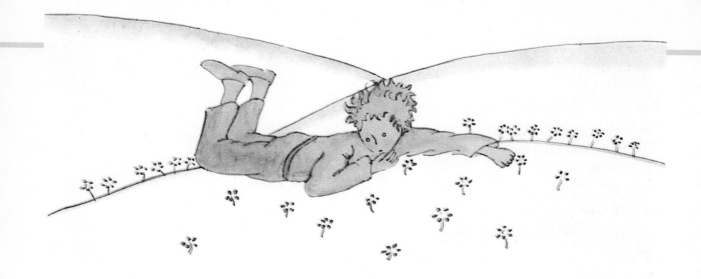

"It is your own fault," said the little prince. "I never wished you any sort of harm; but you wanted me to tame you. . ."

"Yes, that is so," said the fox.

"But now you are going to cry!" said the little prince.

"Yes, that is so," said the fox.

"Then it has done you no good at all!"

"It has done me good," said the fox, "because of the color of the wheat fields." And then he added:

"Go and look again at the roses. You will understand now that yours is unique in all the world. Then come back to say goodbye to me, and I will make you a present of a secret."

The little prince went away, to look again at the roses.

"You are not at all like my rose," he said. "As yet you are nothing. No one has tamed you, and you have tamed no one. You are like my fox when I first knew him. He was only a fox like a hundred thousand other foxes. But I have made him my friend, and now he is unique in all the world."

And the roses were very much embarrassed.

"You are beautiful, but you are empty," he went on. "One could not die for you. To be sure, an ordinary passerby would think that my rose looked just like you—the rose that belongs to me. But in herself alone she is more important than all the hundreds of you other roses: because it is she that I have watered; because it is she that I have put under the

Reading: Analyze characterization as delineated through a character's thoughts, words, speech patterns, and actions, the narrator's description, and the thoughts, words, and actions of other characters

glass globe; because it is she that I have sheltered behind the screen; because it is for her that I have killed the caterpillars (except the two or three that we saved to become butterflies); because it is she that I have listened to, when she grumbled, or boasted, or even sometimes when she said nothing. Because she is *my* rose."

And he went back to meet the fox.

"Goodbye," said the fox. "And now here is my secret, a very simple secret: It is only with the heart that one can see rightly; what is essential is invisible to the eye."

"What is essential is invisible to the eye," the little prince repeated, so that he would be sure to remember.

sheltered: protected

essential: necessary; cannot do without

"It is the time you have wasted for your rose that makes your rose so important."

"It is the time I have wasted for my rose—" said the little prince, so that he would be sure to remember.

"Men have forgotten this truth," said the fox. "But you must not forget it. You become responsible, forever, for what you have tamed. You are responsible for your rose. . ."

As You Read

1. What makes the little prince's rose special to him?

2. What is the rose like? How can you tell?

3. Think about the prince at the beginning of the story. Has he changed now?

About the Author

Antoine de Saint-Exupéry (1900–1944)

Antoine de Saint-Exupéry was born in Lyon, France. He dreamed of being a naval officer, but instead became a pilot. Some of his experiences during his flights, including his crashes in the desert, are described in his essays and novels.

Reading: Analyze characterization as delineated through a character's thoughts, words, speech patterns, and actions, the narrator's description, and the thoughts, words, and actions of other characters

After You Read

Retell It!

With a partner, retell the story of "The Fox" from different points of view. One of you should be the little prince and the other will be the fox. Tell the other what you observe as you tell the story.

Think, Discuss, Write

Discuss these questions in small groups. Write your answers on a separate sheet of paper.

1. **Word analysis**   How does the fox define the word *rite*?

2. **Recall details**   Why did the fox want to be tamed?

3. **Tone**   Describe the fox's *tone* as he defines the word *tame*.

4. **Details**   What is the secret the fox shares with the prince?

5. **Make inferences**   Why is the fox's friendship important to the little prince?

6. **Compare and contrast**   What differences do you notice between the two characters? How are they the same?

7. **Character development**   How have the characters changed by the end of the story?

What's Your Opinion?

Do you agree with what the fox said about friendship? Work with a partner and list points you agree with. Make a persuasive presentation, or

A red fox.

Speaking Applications: Deliver persuasive presentations; state a clear position in support of an argument or proposal; describe the points in support of the argument and employ well-articulated evidence

argument, to your class about what friendship is. Create a list of reasons to support your argument.

Launch into Grammar

Prepositions   Prepositions are words used together with other words—usually nouns and pronouns—to describe *when, where,* or *how.* Prepositions include *at, in, by, under, on, over, below, with, through, until, up, during,* and many others.

In sentences, prepositions are used in phrases such as: *under the apple tree, over the rainbow, with a smile, at the beginning, during the night.* With a partner, find the prepositions in each sentence.

1. Come and play with me.

2. To me, you will be unique in all the world.

3. Are there hunters on that planet?

4. The fox gazed at the little prince for a long time.

Extend: Look for prepositions in your readings from other classes.

 For more practice with prepositions, use page 19 of the Student Workbook.

Mars, the fourth planet.

Connecting to
Science

What was the little prince's home planet? It could have been Mars. Mars is the fourth planet from the Sun. It rotates every 24.6 hours, but it takes 687 of our hours to complete a rotation around the sun. Because the tilt of Mars is almost the same as Earth's, the planet may have four seasons. It also has an atmosphere, although it is thinner than ours.

Written Standards: Identify and correctly use prepositional phrases

Launch into Word Analysis

Words with more than one meaning Many words have two or more meanings.

> "You must be very *patient*," replied the fox.
> She is a *patient* at the hospital.

Both sentences use the word *patient.* But in the first sentence, it means "able to stay calm." In the second sentence, it means "a person cared for by a doctor." With a partner, write down on a separate sheet of paper the meanings for the words in italic (slanted) type in the following sentences.

> What does that *mean*?
> The girl was *mean* to her brother.

> I shall *show* you how happy I am!
> The *show* starts at five o'clock.

> You are not at all like my *rose.*
> The sun *rose* in the morning.

 For more practice with words that have multiple meanings, use page 20 of the Student Workbook.

Study Tip

Use notes to help you learn vocabulary. Write a word you want to learn in your Vocabulary Log and put it in a place where you will see it several times a day.

Reading: Distinguish and interpret words with multiple meanings

Launch into Writing

Write a character sketch   Creating characters is an important part of writing a story. The characters you write about should seem like real people. They should be interesting and believable. To write a character sketch, answer questions such as the ones below.

1. What does this character look like? Is he or she tall or short? What strikes your eye when you look at this person?

2. How does this character act? What kinds of things does he or she do or say? Describe the character's personality. Is this character quiet? Talkative? Serious? Silly? Sad? Loveable? Make your description as lively and meaningful as possible.

3. What kinds of interests, attitudes, and drives does this character have? What does he or she like and dislike? What does this person think about and care about?

   Write a character sketch of someone you know or don't know on a separate sheet of paper. When you are finished, exchange papers with a classmate. Go over each other's sketch. What can you do to make your sketch better?

 For more practice writing a character sketch, use pages 22–23 of the Student Workbook.

Writing: Write descriptions that use concrete sensory details to present and support unified impressions of people, places, things, or experiences

4

GREG
and
WILLIE

**an excerpt from a
nonfiction book by
Suzanne Haldane**

Background

When Greg became paralyzed, he thought he would
never be able to live a normal life again. Thanks to
the help of his best friend, a capuchin monkey
named Willie, and a lot of hard work on his own part,
Greg has regained the ability to do many things for
himself. Using a mouthstick and a laser, he is able to
use a computer and do an amazing number of tasks.
In this reading selection, you will learn about a very
special kind of friendship.

LEARNING OBJECTIVES

- Articulate the expressed purpose and
  characteristics of different forms of prose
- Identify and use imperatives
- Identify synonyms
- Identify settings

Building Your Vocabulary

Make a chart like that on the top of page 35 on a
separate sheet of paper. Put an X next to the items
you know how to use, the ones you don't
know how to use, and the ones you
would like to learn how to use. Have
your parents, grandparents, or an
older friend make the same chart.
Compare charts with your
classmates.

Reading: Classify grade-appropriate categories of words

Type of Media	Know How To Use	Don't Know How To Use	Want to Learn How To Use
radio			
television			
VCR			
computer			
telephone			
video camera			

Reading Strategy

Distinguish between different forms of prose

Prose can be either nonfiction, a real life story, or fiction (a story that is not real). As you read, think about what type of reading "Greg and Willie" is.

Applying the Reading Strategy

As you read "Greg and Willie," consider the following:

1. Think about who is telling the story.

2. Write down any facts that the author provides.

3. How does the story compare to the other readings in the unit? How is it the same? How is it different?

4. How does the author describe Greg and Willie's surroundings? How does she describe time and place?

Reading: Articulate the expressed purpose and characteristics of different forms of prose

GREG and WILLIE

an excerpt from a nonfiction book by Suzanne Haldane

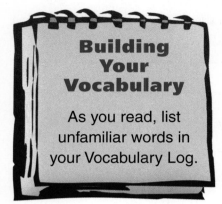

Building Your Vocabulary

As you read, list unfamiliar words in your Vocabulary Log.

As You Read

1. What are Willie's most frequent jobs for Greg?

2. Describe what Willie looks like. What words does the author use to describe her?

On the way to Greg's, Willie sat on the front seat of the car beside her trainer. Every now and then she got up on the back of the seat and looked out the car window. When they arrived at Greg's house, Willie climbed up on her trainer's shoulder and wrapped her tail around the young woman's neck so she wouldn't fall off as they walked into the house.

The trainer placed Willie immediately in her cage, knowing that the confinement would give Willie a sense of security. After a brief discussion with Greg, and a promise to return when the monkey felt at ease, Willie's trainer left.

"For about a week Willie didn't come out of her cage," says Greg. As a means of encouraging her to come out, she was offered food outside her cage. Invariably she grabbed it and ran back inside her safe quarters.

During Willie's period of adjustment, Greg's family gave her a rubber squeaky toy, which she held in her tail. Sometimes she insisted on taking it to bed with her.

Willie appears to be quite comfortable now and knows her routine. Her most frequent jobs are putting Greg's mouthstick back in his mouth when he drops it, serving him drinks, and fetching a book when he lets her know one.

She is a wiry character. Her body almost resembles the animals children make from pipe cleaners. When she's in motion, her quick

invariably: constantly, always
adjustment: getting used to something

Reading: Articulate the expressed purpose and characteristics of different forms of prose

movements are exaggerated by her long arms and legs.

Greg is a determined individual. He insists on doing all that he can for himself. He operates a cassette player, computer, and push-button telephone with his mouthstick. He also uses it to turn the pages of a magazine or book. It's a helpful instrument, but it can easily slip out of his mouth. During long periods of work on the computer, Greg sometimes drops the stick.

When he does, he says, "Willie, fetch stick," and Willie picks it up and puts it back into his mouth.

"You should have seen Willie while she was learning how to give me the mouthstick. It didn't take her very long to get it right, but sometimes she put it in her own mouth. It was a funny scene!"

Greg is completing his education by computer. He had a specially designed tray fitted onto his display terminal so that Willie can help him when he uses his computer. He points to a floppy disk with his mouthstick and then taps the tray.

Willie picks up the disk and drops it into the tray. Greg uses his mouthstick to push the disk into the disk drive. Then he's ready to work.

On his worktable, Greg has a stand that supports open books and magazines. One side of the stand is hinged so that it folds over and lies flat when not in use.

On top of the stand is a round magnet. Greg's magazines are fastened inside cardboard folders.

display terminal: a computer monitor

Reading: Articulate the expressed purpose and characteristics of different forms of prose

At the top of each folder there is a metal disk. On command, Willie fetches a magazine and matches the metal disk on the folder to the magnet on the stand. The magnet holds the folder in place.

Next, she sets the stand in the upright position and flips the magazine open for Greg to read.

When Greg is thirsty he asks Willie to serve him a drink. Greg says, "Willie, door." Willie goes to the small refrigerator and opens the door. Greg aims the laser at a bottle and says, "Willie, fetch." Willie takes out the plastic juice container the light beam is hitting and carries it over to Greg's worktable. She puts the bottle into a holder anchored on the table, then unscrews the lid. Next she inserts a straw. Greg wheels himself into position in front of the straw and drinks.

Occasionally Willie feeds Greg with a spoon, but usually Greg prefers human help for that. Willie sometimes tips the spoon over. And at times she forgets and feeds herself instead of Greg.

Willie has been taught to open the door of her cage, go in, and close the door behind her. If Greg wants her to go in, he says, "Willie, cage," and she obeys. When the cage door closes, it automatically locks.

At bedtime, Greg says, "Willie, cage," and she goes in. When the room is dark and she's ready to sleep, she pulls a large bath towel over herself and settles down for eight to twelve hours of rest.

laser: a tiny beam of light

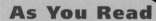

As You Read

1. What does Greg say to Willie when he is thirsty?

2. Why does Greg prefer to be fed by a human hand?

Reading: Articulate the expressed purpose and characteristics of different forms of prose

There can be some unpredictable moments with a monkey living at home. Once when everyone was out of the house and the door to Willie's cage wasn't properly latched, she got out. "Willie is well fed, but she always knows where the food is," Greg says. "On that day, my brother came home and found her perched high on one of the beams in the living room. Of course he was shocked. He put Willie back in her cage and went into the kitchen. Then he was really surprised. It was a mess. The refrigerator door was open and there were smashed eggs all over the floor. All the cabinet doors were ajar and there were squashed bananas, pieces of marshmallows, and cookie crumbs on the counter. You'd better believe we always check to make sure her lock is secure when we leave the house now!"

Greg is proud of Willie and all that she can do. "She's a lot more to me than just helping hands," he says. "I spend all day, every day, in my wheelchair. One of my parents will drive me in my van to visit friends and go to ball games or movies, but a lot more of my time is spent at home than it used to be— before my accident.

Reading: Articulate the expressed purpose and characteristics of different forms of prose

"Willie gives me something to think about besides myself. When she's out of her cage, I'm always looking around to find out where she is and what she's doing."

Greg doesn't take Willie out in public. But people with quadriplegia who do take their monkeys to places like parks or shopping centers report that strangers pay greater attention to them when they are accompanied by their monkeys.

Many people have an inhibition about talking with someone in a wheelchair. They don't know quite what to say, so they don't say anything at all and ignore both the person and the chair. When a person who has quadriplegia is with a monkey, the stranger can focus attention on the monkey until he or she feels comfortable about looking at and talking directly to the person. "What is the monkey's name? What does the monkey eat? How long have you had the monkey?" These are the questions that are usually asked first. Perhaps a few more questions follow; then, before stranger and quadriplegic know it, they're having a conversation.

Greg still has the friends he had before his accident, but he's noticed that when he makes new friends, his monkey is a great help in easing the awkwardness that exists in any new friendship.

"Willie's fun to play with. She really enjoys games," says Greg. "My friends like to play catch or wrestle with her and give her treats."

quadriplegia: a condition in which a person is paralyzed in both arms and both legs

inhibition: fear

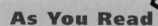

As You Read

1. How does Willie help Greg make new friends?

2. Why would Greg rather have Willie than a robot?

Reading: Articulate the expressed purpose and characteristics of different forms of prose

There's an inseparable connection between a monkey and a person who has quadriplegia. Greg says, "If I've been out of the house, Willie is always excited and glad to see me again when I return. She looks straight at me and makes a chattering sound—a friendly greeting monkey-style. There's a real tight bond between us. From time to time, she grooms my hair—a real sign of trust and affection."

The Helping Hands organization knows how strong bonds can be. Many months after one person with quadriplegia died of a heart attack, his monkey still kissed the photograph of him that his wife kept on the bureau.

"People say to me, 'Why don't you get a robot to help you?' But did you ever see a robot that could be tender and make you laugh?" asks Greg. "Willie takes good care of me. But she's also a good friend. Life wouldn't be nearly as much fun without her."

tight bond: close relationship

Connecting to Science

Every year almost 11,000 Americans injure their spinal cords. Half of these people are between the ages of 16 and 30. Many of them spend their entire adult lives without movement in their arms or legs. You can protect yourself from spinal cord injuries. Wear your seatbelt whenever you ride in a car and wear safety gear when you play sports.

About the Author
Suzanne Haldane (b. 1946)
Suzanne Haldane is the author and illustrator of many children's books, including *Lakota Hoop Dancers* and *Painting Faces*. She lives in Jaffrey, New Hampshire.

Reading: Articulate the expressed purpose and characteristics of different forms of prose

Retell It!

Work in a small group. Willie helps Greg read a magazine. The steps he has to go through are scrambled below. Arrange them in the correct order on a separate sheet of paper.

_____ Willie matches the metal disk on the folder to the magnet on the stand.

_____ Willie fetches a magazine.

_____ Willie sets the stand in the upright position.

_____ She flips the magazine open.

_____ Greg gives a command.

Think, Discuss, Write

Discuss these questions in small groups. Write your answers on a separate piece of paper.

1. **Recall details**   What is the name of Greg's monkey?

2. **Recall details**   How does Greg operate machines such as the computer or telephone?

3. **Recall details**   Why does Greg need a monkey as a helper?

4. **Point of view**   If Willie could talk, what would she say about her job and friendship with Greg?

5. **Make inferences**   Do you think a monkey is an easy pet to have? Why might the monkey be difficult as a pet?

6. **Cause and effect**   How does Willie change Greg's relationship with strangers?

Monkeys can be more than companions.

Reading: Identify and analyze recurrent themes across works; Reading: Articulate the expressed purpose and characteristics of different forms of prose

7. Connect themes Think about the fox's statement in the last reading, "You become responsible for what you tame." Is Willie now tame in the same way the fox is tame in *The Little Prince*?

What's Your Opinion?

Which of the four readings in this unit did you enjoy most? Make a bar graph that shows which selection you liked the most and which you liked the least. Compare your graph with the graphs of other students in your class.

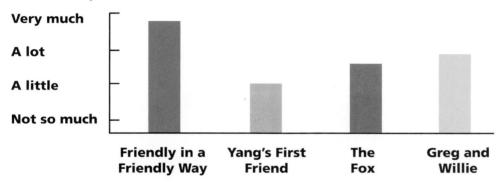

Friendly in a Friendly Way	**Yang's First Friend**	**The Fox**	**Greg and Willie**

Very much — A lot — A little — Not so much

Launch into Grammar

Imperatives   *Imperatives* are used to give orders, suggestions, instruction, advice, and warnings. For example, when Greg says, "Willie, door," he means, "*Open* the door."

Find other examples of imperatives in the story and write sentences, following the example above, on a separate sheet of paper.

 For more practice with imperatives, use page 27 of the Student Workbook.

Capuchin monkey.

Greg and Willie 43

Launch into Word Analysis

Synonyms   Words that have similar meanings are called **synonyms.** Take a look at some of the synonyms listed below.

get, fetch	home, house	jobs, tasks
seat, chair	motion, movement	safe, secure

With a partner, find a synonym for each of the following words from the story. Write your words on a separate sheet of paper.

eat	rest	help
brief	arrived	pages

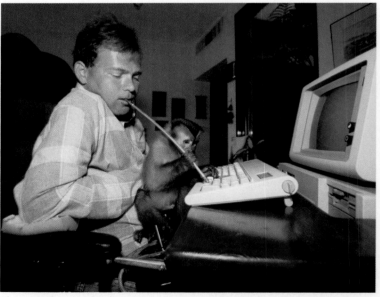

The monkey helps the man use the stick to type with his mouth.

Reading: Clarify word meanings through the use of definition; Reading: Apply knowledge of synonyms to determine the meaning of words

Launch into Writing

Setting   The author writes about Greg and Willie's surroundings. She does this so that the reader can imagine and better understand the situation. The description of time and place in any piece of writing is called the **setting.**

Imagine a special place; it could be a location in your house or school, or a town that you have visited. Write a paragraph that describes that place. Begin your paragraph with the following phrase:

_____ *is one of the most* _____ *places that I have ever been.*

Here is an example:

A student completes a writing assignment.

> *Ixtapa, Zihuatanejo*
>
> *Ixtapa, Zihuatanejo is one of the most beautiful places that I have ever been. The beaches in Ixtapa have sand as smooth as silk. Because of its beauty, it's a great place to go and relax at the beach. But, Ixtapa is also lots of fun.*

 For more practice establishing setting, use pages 30–31 of the Student Workbook.

Writing: Create a single paragraph: Develop a topic sentence, and include simple supporting facts and details

Tell a Story

You have read two narratives in this unit. A narrative is a piece of writing that tells a story and includes **conflict** (story problem), **rising action** (events that lead to the story's turning point), **climax** (the turning point of the story), **falling action** (events that follow the climax), and **resolution** (the end of the story). This series of events is called the story's **plot.**

Form small groups to participate in a storytelling activity. What will you tell a story about?

Step One: Plan Your Story

1. As a group, discuss your ideas and your audience. Decide which idea you will use. Consider the following:

- What kind of story will interest your audience?

- How will you develop your story?

- What point of view will you use?

2. Make an outline. List setting, characters, the story conflict, the rising action, the climax, and the resolution. You will use this outline to tell the story in your own words.

3. Divide the story up into parts and assign one for each student in the group. Mark each person's section on the outline clearly.

Step Two: Practice Your Story

1. Practice telling the story.

2. Use gestures, facial expressions, and varying tones of voice that will help convey the story's meaning.

3. Record or videotape your story. Discuss ways to improve your work.

4. Use the Speaking Checklist to review other groups' stories.

Writing: Create multiple-paragraph narrative compositions: Establish and develop a situation or plot, describe the setting, and present an ending

Step Three:
Tell Your Story

Once you have practiced telling your story, you are ready to present it to the class. Assign one student in your group to answer questions students may have about the setting, plot, or characters.

Step Four:
Evaluate Your Story

Ask your classmates whether your story interested them. Invite them to ask questions or share other ideas they have. What suggestions did they have for improvement?

Record Your Final Story

Add a tape of your story to the classroom listening center. Listen to your own and others' tapes. Check out a tape to share at home with family members.

Speaking Checklist

✔ Speak slowly and clearly.

✔ Use expression and appropriate tone of voice.

✔ Use appropriate body language and gestures.

✔ Make eye contact with your audience.

Writing: Create multiple-paragraph narrative compositions: Establish and develop a situation or plot, describe the setting, and present an ending

Write a Fictional Narrative

In this unit, you have been reading about different friendships. Write a fictional narrative about friendship. Begin by introducing the setting and characters. Use actions and dialogue to show conflict between the characters. End with the result of the characters' actions and a conclusion.

Here is an example:

Pierre and Gigi

Once upon a time, in a small town in France, there were two kids named Gigi and Pierre. Pierre was not very good at sports, but he always tried everything. Gigi, however, was very good at sports, but she would rather knit than go ice skating or play hockey.

When Pierre decided to try out for the hockey team, Gigi laughed and said, "Ooh la la. You're going to try out for hockey? Ha, ha, ha. Everyone knows that they will take me over you any day. I suggest you pick another sport!"

After tryouts ended, the coaches made a small speech. "We have selected our team not because of the people who are the best skaters, but because we are looking for interested, enthusiastic members who are eager to learn!" When they went to check and see whether they made the team, Pierre's name was on the list, and Gigi's was not.

Writing: Write narratives: Relate observations of an experience; Provide a context, use sensory details, and provide insight into why the experience is memorable

1. Pre-write

Decide on your purpose and audience. Who will your readers be? What lesson do you want your story to convey? Brainstorm traits and actions to support your purpose.

2. Draft

Follow these steps to organize your fictional narrative.

A. Introduce your setting and characters.

B. Set up a conflict.

C. Show actions and results.

D. End with a lesson.

Refer to any notes you jotted down to guide you as you draft your fictional narrative.

3. Revise

Reread your draft and ask yourself these questions:

- Have I given the time and place?
- Have I told the events in the order they occurred?
- Have I described my characters with strong, colorful words?
- Is the lesson clear?

Consider your answers to these questions as you revise your narrative. Ask a classmate to answer these same questions about your narrative. Make any additional changes based on your classmate's feedback.

4. Edit and Proofread

Proofread your revised narrative. Check sentence punctuation, capitalization, and spelling. Look in the dictionary to verify your spelling.

5. Publish

Make a book. Follow these steps:

A. Give your story a title.

B. Decide which part of the narrative should be on each page. Then, recopy or type the text for each page and glue it onto pre-cut poster board.

C. Make an illustration for each page that goes with the text.

D. Bind the pages together and display your book with your classmates'.

Writing: Revise original drafts to improve sequence and provide more descriptive detail

Interview

Project Goal

In this unit you read about different friendships. In this project you will identify the most important characteristics of a true friend.

1. Work in small groups. Interview six people. Be sure to interview people of different genders, ages, and ethnic backgrounds. Ask them to list the five most important qualities of a true friend. Fill in a chart like the one below for each person you interview.

Name: Maria Panico
Age: 14
Qualities:
1. loyalty
2. sense of humor

2. Analyze your findings. List all the qualities that you collected that are unique. Add any characteristics that you think have been left out. Using your list, write a description of the perfect friend.

Design a poster that lists the qualities of your friend. Find pictures that illustrate these qualities in a magazine or on the Internet.

Select a member of your group to present your perfect friend model to the rest of the class. Convince your audience that your friend is a wonderful person!

Words to Know

- characteristics
- gender
- background
- ethnic

Writing: Use traditional structures for conveying information

Read More About Friendship

Choose one or more of the following books to write about. Write down in your Reading Log what books you read and your opinion of each. Ask yourself these questions:

1. What kind of friendship did you read about?
2. Are the characters learning more about the meaning of friendship?
3. What did this book teach you about how to treat and help others?

Fiction

Freak the Mighty by Rodman Philbrick.

A physically disabled boy befriends a boy with learning disabilities and together they become "Freak the Mighty." The boys enjoy adventures together based on the legends of King Arthur's Round Table.

American Dream by Lisa Banim.

Jeannie and Amy, who is Japanese-American, are best friends. The attack on Pearl Harbor dramatically changes the girls' lives when Amy and her family must move to a government internment camp.

Nonfiction

Trust and Betrayal: Real Life Stories of Friends and Enemies by Janet Bode.

The author interviews teenagers about their friendships. Real stories of reaching out, establishing ties, fighting and making up paint a complex picture of teen friendships.

If You Could Be My Friend: Letters of Mervet Akram Sha'Ban and Galit Fink by Mervet Akram Sha'Ban and Galit Fink, edited by Litsa Boudalika.

Two teenagers, one Israeli and one Palestinian, belong to ethnic and religious groups at odds with each other. As they write to each other, they discover that friendship can overcome prejudice.

Reading: Compare and contrast information on the same topic

UNIT 2
Courage

"Courage is knowing
what not to fear."
—Plato (Greek philosopher and writer,
ca. 427–348 B.C.E.)

Discuss the Theme

Being Courageous

Courage can take many forms. It can be the courage to stand up for your rights or the rights of others such as in "The Last Princess," and in "Emma Garcia: Community Organizer at age 16." Courage may also be the willingness to face your own fears as in "Call It Courage," a story about a boy's frightening experience and his efforts to make a new beginning. In *She's Wearing a Dead Bird on Her Head!*, you will read about women who have the courage to take an unpopular position. Sometimes we are called upon to do things that frighten us, and sometimes we choose to do these things. Any time we face our own fears, we show courage.

- What does the word courage mean to you?
- Who do you know who is courageous?
- What situations have you faced that required you to be courageous?

WRITING FOCUS:
Persuasive Composition

Before You Read

5

the **Last Princess**

**an excerpt from a
nonfiction book
by Fay Stanley**

Background

Princess Ka'iulani (1875–1898) was the last princess
of Hawai'i. You will read about how she tried to save
her country from being annexed by the United
States. When she heard that Americans were trying
to overthrow Hawai'i's monarchy, Ka'iulani went to
Washington to present her country's case to the
president of the United States.

LEARNING OBJECTIVES

- Learn to take notes
- Learn to use pronouns and antecedents
- Learn to use prefixes
- Learn to write a proposal

Building Your Vocabulary

1. To understand what occurred in Hawai'i in the
   1890s, it is necessary to understand words that
   have to do with different types of government and
   political change. Look at the list of words below.
   Use a dictionary to find the meaning of any words
   you do not know.

royal	revolution	revolutionaries
kingdom	representative	monarch
nation	Senate	queen
statesmen	Congress	king
rights	throne	
president	independence	

Reading: Use a dictionary to learn the meaning and other features of unknown words

2. With a partner, create on a separate sheet of paper your own word web like the one to the right. Use the list from page 54. You may use the same word more than once. Share your webs with your class.

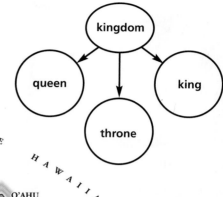

Reading Strategy

Take notes   When you read nonfiction, taking notes can help you organize and keep track of the information you read. First, notes should be brief. Second, notes should be written in a form that is useful to you. And finally, the information in your notes should be clear and easy to understand.

Applying the Reading Strategy

Follow these steps to take notes using a dialogue journal format:

1. As you read, record the key facts, figures, and ideas. Shorten all names, explanations, and lengthy descriptions into a few phrases or sentences.

2. Get to the heart of each subject you are taking notes on. Summarize complicated paragraphs by focusing on the major ideas and events that they include. Don't waste words. Ask yourself: "What is the main point here and how can I express it in the fewest number of words?"

3. Organize your notes into an outline if you prefer. List major points after Roman numeral headings (I, II, III), and supporting information after capital letter headings (A, B, C) and standard number headings (1, 2, 3).

4. You might also choose to organize your notes in a written summary. This summary expresses most of the same ideas that your outline included, yet it uses a paragraph form.

Reading: Clarify an understanding of text by creating outlines, logical notes, summaries, or reports

the Last Princess

an excerpt from
a nonfiction book by Fay Stanley

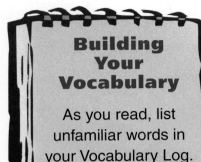

As You Read

1. Who is the narrator?
2. What is the point of view?
3. What do the words "she conquered the American press" mean?

Once she had decided on her course, Ka'iulani did not waver from it. Before leaving England in February, she spoke of her cause to newspaper reporters and won their hearts completely. A few weeks later, when she and her guardian docked in New York, she conquered the American press, too. The reporters wrote about her delicate beauty, her talent for music, art, and languages, and her manners—those of a "born aristocrat." And when she read her short, prepared statement many had tears in their eyes.

In a quiet voice, she told the reporters how it felt to arrive alone "upon the shores . . . where she thought to receive a royal welcome" to find enemies working to take away her kingdom, to "leave her without a home or a name or a nation." She finished by saying, "Today, I, a poor, weak girl with not one of my people near me and all these . . . statesmen against me, have strength to stand up for the rights of my people. Even now I can hear their wail in my heart and it gives me strength and courage."

When Ka'iulani finally arrived in Washington, President and Mrs. Cleveland were deeply impressed by her courage and dignity. The president assured the princess that he would see justice done to her and her people. He announced that a special investigator would sail to Hawai'i immediately to

aristocrat: a person named as noble by a king or queen

Reading: Clarify an understanding of text by creating outlines, logical notes, summaries, or reports

report on the true situation there. This was the happiest news Ka'iulani had received since the revolution. Believing she had successfully accomplished her mission, she felt free to return to England.

But after the hectic month in the United States, it was hard for Ka'iulani to settle back to her schoolgirl routine. She waited anxiously for news from home. It finally came in August. The president's representative was back from Hawai'i and had reported to the Senate that a "wrong had been done to the Hawaiians, who were overwhelmingly opposed to annexation." The president then urged that Congress find a way to restore the queen to her throne.

It seemed to Ka'iulani that she had won. She, "a poor, weak girl," had helped save her aunt's throne and her people's independence. But her joy and triumph at the good news was short lived.

The *haoles* refused to disband their new government, and the president was unwilling to send American troops to force the *haoles* to step down. The only help he could give the Hawaiians was to block their country's annexation as long as he was president.

A group of outraged and disappointed young Hawaiians decided to take matters into their own hands. If the United States government could not restore their queen, they would do it themselves—by force!

As You Read

1. Are the Hawaiians in favor of annexation?
2. Do you think Princess Ka'iulani has accomplished her mission? Why or why not?
3. What do you think "take matters into their own hands" means?
4. What is the goal of the young Hawaiians?

annexation: the capture or purchase of a country or territory by another country

haoles: those who are not descended from the original Polynesian people of Hawai'i

Reading: Clarify an understanding of text by creating outlines, logical notes, summaries, or reports

Queen Lili'oukalani.

For months, these fiery young men planned their revolt. They secretly shipped in guns from California, which they buried on the beach at night. On the evening of January 6, 1895, they gathered together and prepared to storm Honolulu the next day. But because a spy in their group told the authorities about the plan, and because the young men were poorly trained and armed, they were quickly put down. About two hundred Hawaiians were arrested, among them many friends and relatives of Ka'iulani's.

Reading: Clarify an understanding of text by creating outlines, logical notes, summaries, or reports

To save the lives of these revolutionaries, the queen agreed to sign a document in which she formally gave up the throne. But the queen's punishment was not complete. She was also imprisoned in her own palace, tried for treason, and given a sentence of five years at hard labor plus a fine of five thousand dollars!

Later, this savage sentence was lightened. But the monarchy was finished. Hawaiian kings and queens would never again rule over their beloved people.

In these last years, many Hawaiians had been robbed of their land and their right to vote, and now they had lost their own government. They were now a minority in their own country, outnumbered by immigrants from the Orient and the *haoles*. White man's diseases had caused the death of many of these independent, good-hearted people.

At the bitter news from Hawai'i, Ka'iulani put aside her own dismay and grief and thought of her people. She knew in her heart that her place now was at home.

treason: an illegal attempt to overthrow a government
the Orient: the countries lying east of Europe; the Far East

As You Read

1. Why does the queen agree to give up her throne?
2. Do you think that the queen has committed treason? Why or why not?
3. What does it mean to be "a minority in their own country"?
4. What does "savage sentence" mean in the story?

About the Author
Fay Stanley

Fay Stanley has written several detective stories for adults. *The Last Princess* is the only book she has written for young people. This book is illustrated by her daughter, Diane Stanley. Diane Stanley is an award-winning writer and illustrator of many books for children and young adults.

Reading: Clarify an understanding of text by creating outlines, logical notes, summaries, or reports

After You Read

Retell It!

With a partner, retell the story of Ka'iulani in the form of an interview. One of you should be the interviewer, and the other the princess. Present your interview to the class.

Think, Discuss, Write

Work with a partner. Write your answers on a separate sheet of paper.

1. **Recall details**   Why was it hard for Ka'iulani to get back to her regular school routine?

2. **Recall details**   On what day did young Hawaiians decide to storm Honolulu?

3. **Make inferences**   How do you think the queen felt after she gave up the throne?

4. **Structure**   How does the structure of this selection differ from a first-person narrative?

5. **Theme**   What is a major theme of this reading?

6. **Sentence analysis**   What clues did the author provide to allow you to make predictions about what would happen?

7. **Compare and contrast**   Compare Ka'iulani's idea of "home" with your own idea of "home."

What's Your Opinion?

Did you like this selection? Fill in a chart like the one shown and compare it with your classmates' charts.

Palm trees.

Study Tip

Try never to miss classes; borrowing someone else's notes should be a last resort. In class, be a good listener. Don't be afraid or embarrassed to ask questions in class. Unless your teacher has specifically asked not to be interrupted, put up your hand as soon as you don't understand something. Otherwise, you may forget to ask, or you may become more confused.

Reading: Recall major points in the text and make or modify predictions

What I Liked About This Reading	What I Didn't Like About This Reading
I thought Ka'iulani was very brave	*Too many facts to remember*

Launch into Grammar

Pronouns and antecedents **Pronouns** are words that take the place of nouns or other pronouns. The word, or words, that the pronoun refers to is called an **antecedent.**

> **Example:** The *president* came. The princess talked to *him*. (pronoun: *him*, antecedent: *president*)

With a partner, identify each antecedent of the underlined pronoun in the sentences. Use a separate sheet of paper.

1. Many Hawaiians had been robbed of their land. Now <u>they</u> lost their right to vote.

2. The queen agreed to sign a document in which <u>she</u> gave up the throne.

3. It seemed to Ka'iulani that <u>she</u> had won.

> **Extend:** As you read for your other subjects, look for pronouns and their antecedents.

The Hawaiian State Capitol.

 For more practice with pronouns, complete page 35 in the Student Workbook.

The Last Princess   61

Reading: Make clear references between pronouns and antecedents; Reading: Use pronouns correctly in writing and speaking

A portion of Hawaiian coastline.

Writing Tip

When you write about a serious topic, be careful not to use casual language. Avoid using phrases like **so anyway, you know,** and **whatever**!

Launch into Word Analysis

Prefixes   A **prefix** is a word part that attaches to a word root and creates a new word. Prefixes always come *before* the word root. When you recognize prefixes, you can figure out the meaning of new words.

In the reading, several words using the prefix *re* are used. *Re* means *again.*

Look at the four words and their meanings. Write the four words and the number of the correct definition on a separate sheet of paper. Do the meanings help you understand these words better?

report   **1.** to make something go somewhere again

receive   **2.** to take something again

return   **3.** to carry news again

restore   **4.** to put someone in the possession of something again

For more practice with prefixes, use page 36 in the Student Workbook.

Reading: Use knowledge of Greek, Latin, and Anglo-Saxon roots and affixes to understand content-area vocabulary;
Reading: Use knowledge of prefixes to determine the meaning of words

Launch into Writing

State a proposal   A **proposal** is a formal offer that one person or group makes to another; one side says to the other: "I will promise *this* if you will promise *that.*" Well thought-out proposals can help solve very difficult problems. The secret to writing a good proposal is to use a balanced approach. Think about the other side's needs as well as your own.

> Since Hawaii is now a part of the United States, it would not be possible to restore the Hawaiian king or queen to power. However, many Hawaiians today still have a fondness for the kings and queens of the past. In honor of those days, we hereby propose that January 6th be named Queen and King's Day, so we can celebrate Hawaii's proud history.

Write a proposal for something you are interested in on a sheet of paper. Consider all sides of the issue before you begin writing.

For more practice stating clear positions, use page 38–39 of the Student Workbook.

6

Before You Read

Background

It's easy to complain about problems, but it takes courage to do something about them. In this chapter, you will learn about one girl who decided to improve conditions at her high school and in her community, and for teens in general. Think about problems in your school that you might change.

Emma García: Community Organizer at Age 16

an excerpt from a nonfiction book by Marlene Targ Brill

LEARNING OBJECTIVES

- Learn how to summarize
- Learn to use subjects and verbs
- Learn how to recognize suffixes
- Learn how to provide supporting facts

Building Your Vocabulary

1. Words like *first, next, then,* and *finally* reveal time order or sequence. They are used to describe the time order in which an event or events occurred. Or, they might be used to tell you the order in which you should do something. Some time-order words are:

first	while	when
before	soon	later
meanwhile	after	then

2. With a partner, create a time line of what you recently did to help someone. Use five of the words in the list. These words will help your

Reading: Analyze text that is organized in sequential or chronological order

readers understand the order of when these events occurred. Begin with **first**. Write the timeline on a separate sheet of paper.

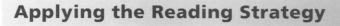

First

Reading Strategy

Write summaries of reading materials   A **summary** is a brief rundown that includes all of the important ideas and key conclusions that are contained in a longer work. A summary should be easy to read, written in your own words, and brief. Summaries should include only the highlights and major points.

Applying the Reading Strategy

1. Read the article about Emma Garcia carefully. Make mental notes of key points and major ideas that the article presents.

2. Read each section that you are going to summarize once again. Then summarize the section in a short sentence or two.

Include only major events, points, and ideas.

3. Continue to summarize, section by section. Now, go over the summary you've written and make sure that it reads smoothly and clearly. Get rid of any extra information you included!

Writing: Write summaries of reading materials: Include the main ideas and most significant details, use the student's own words, and reflect underlying meaning

Emma Garcia: Community Organizer at Age 16

an excerpt from a nonfiction book by Marlene Targ Brill

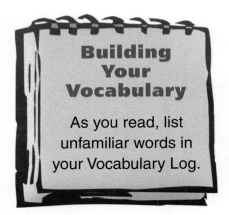

Building Your Vocabulary

As you read, list unfamiliar words in your Vocabulary Log.

As You Read

1. Summarize what you just read. What are the most important facts and events?

2. Explain why conflicts between young people are often deadly today.

3. Does the author think that kids are wilder today than their parents were?

4. Why does Emma's family have to move often?

Every generation of adults claims that kids are wilder, care less about their community, or are more violent than kids "in our day." Adults tend to forget the neighborhood turf wars that went on in most cities in every generation. They overlook how kids naturally tease each other and argue in the streets, playgrounds, and alleys. The difference now, however, is that many more conflicts between young people turn deadly. Guns kill more teens than AIDS, cancer, and heart disease combined. Emma Garcia and several students at Oakland High School in California wanted to reverse that trend.

Emma came from a loving family, but one that struggled economically. Until Emma was four, her parents moved frequently in order to find work. In 1976, the family migrated from Baja, in Mexico, to the Oakland area.

Emma spoke only Spanish until she learned English in the first grade. As the oldest of four children, she became the family translator. Emma helped her parents prepare tax forms and other documents in English, a big responsibility for someone so young. The family proudly maintained their Mexican customs. But her parents always emphasized the importance of school and of contributing to the community, wherever they lived.

turf: an area people claim as their own territory

Writing: Write summaries of reading materials: Include the main ideas and most significant details, use the student's own words, and reflect underlying meaning

Emma and her brothers and sister often joined other children in the streets of their diverse Oakland neighborhood. They spent many evenings playing hide-and-seek in the dark. By the time Emma was nine, however, the neighborhood had changed. Several large companies had moved, leaving about twenty percent of the adults without jobs. Drug dealers entered the once-safe neighborhood. With the drug trade came violence and guns. Soon, Emma and her friends feared going out at night.

As a teenager, the effects of neighborhood violence affected Emma's school life. Emma was upset that her school never held dances or extracurricular activities that other teens enjoyed. Teachers feared drive-by shootings before and after school events. They worried that school functions were magnets for drug dealers. And a dangerous practice arose— shooting guns into the air at school dances.

Budget cuts further hurt local school districts. Some classes were eliminated, as were arts and sports programs. Poor neighborhoods like Emma's were hit hardest. Emma and her friends had nothing to keep themselves busy when they were not in class. Kids who were bored with schoolwork had no other activities that attracted them to school. The result was a sixty-percent dropout rate at Oakland High School. Drugs and violence overtook the school. Forty percent of the girls at the school got pregnant.

As You Read

1. How does Emma's neighborhood change? What causes the change?

2. Why does Emma's school never have activities after school?

Emma Garcia: Community Organizer at Age 16   67

Emma set her goals higher than most of her classmates. She was a good student and the editor of the school newspaper. Her enthusiasm for learning earned her a place in a special school media program. She taught Sunday school and was involved in many church activities. "The activities and the good people I met gave me a strong sense of working for change in the community," she says.

But these successes couldn't erase Emma's sadness about what was happening to her friends. The murder rate for young people in Oakland was soaring, and several of Emma's friends were killed. After a record-breaking year of killings in her high school, sixteen-year-old Emma knew something had to be done.

So did the Oakland Unified School District. The school asked Deanne Calhoun (who worked for an injury-prevention group) to work with students in Emma's media program. Emma and seven classmates formed the core of what evolved into "Teens on Target," the first youth violence-prevention program in the United States.

Part of Emma's class produced a videotape. Meanwhile, Emma helped devise a questionnaire to ask other kids what they thought about violence in their neighborhoods. The survey brought an overwhelming response. Kids said they

As You Read

1. What convinces Emma that something has to be done about the guns in her community?

2. What is the name of organization that develops out of the media program's project?

record-breaking: becoming greater than the past

Writing: Write summaries of reading materials: Include the main ideas and most significant details, use the student's own words, and reflect underlying meaning

desperately wanted to talk. Mostly, they wanted to talk with other kids whom they trusted, not to adults.

Emma's class decided to organize a conference in the Bay Area as a forum to explore ideas further. Emma spent the summer before her senior year at the media center. She worked with local school and community organizations to brainstorm about what to include in the conference. The fall 1989 conference covered four areas of violence: family; gang and street; gun; and drug and alcohol.

More than two hundred kids from the San Francisco Bay Area attended the conference. They represented middle- and high-school students from a variety of ethnic and social backgrounds. Some were teens who had been arrested and attended as part of their parole agreements.

At the conference, the teenagers agreed that violence had taken over their neighborhoods, and that something must be done. They said that young people needed more information about the effects of guns and violence. They needed to learn how to resolve conflicts peacefully. Moreover, they wanted to talk with their peers about these issues, not with adults.

As a result of the conference, Emma Garcia took it upon herself to educate students. She received training from Youth Alive, a public

forum: public meeting or discussion

As You Read

1. Summarize what you just read. What are the most important facts or events?

2. What four areas of violence are covered in the 1989 conference?

Writing: Write summaries of reading materials: Include the main ideas and most significant details, use the student's own words, and reflect underlying meaning

health agency. With her teachers' permission, she gave presentations in junior-high and high-school classes three to four times over a three-week period. More than fifty similarly trained students joined Emma.

Teens on Target soon expanded to Los Angeles, explaining violence prevention to nearly a thousand kids a year. Adults in state and local agencies were surprised that kids like Emma had so many good ideas about such serious issues. In 1990, Emma attended a national conference for public health officials. She and Teens on Target brought the message that kids were dying from more serious threats than a lack of bicycle helmets. Her group gained much-needed attention from the public health workers.

In Oakland, Emma urged lawmakers to expand and enforce laws banning billboards advertising liquor and cigarettes near schools. She was angry that her classmates could get guns, liquor, and drugs near school, but had to take a bus to buy school supplies. Emma also appealed to voters in the 1995 election to set aside one percent of the state budget for youth issues.

Emma graduated from high school and college. But she stayed committed to Teens on Target and ending youth violence. Emma started as a Teens

Writing: Write summaries of reading materials: Include the main ideas and most significant details, use the student's own words, and reflect underlying meaning

on Target rookie, then became a trainer, and then became program director. She coordinated school presentations and special projects for younger kids. She wrote a training manual for incoming Teens on Target role models and organized news conferences.

"The community has a lot to do with what individuals do with their lives, whether they become college students or drug dealers," Emma stresses. "It's important for young people to contribute to the community, and for the community to care about its young people. Kids have to speak out!"

rookie: a beginner or new person

As You Read

1. What is the important message that Emma brings to the national conference for public health officials?

2. List what Emma does after she graduates from high school and college.

3. What should the community do for its young people? What should young people do for their communities?

About the Author
Marlene Targ Brill

Marlene Targ Brill lives in Illinois with her husband and children. Before becoming an author, she was a teacher. She has written many fiction and nonfiction books.

Writing: Write summaries of reading materials: Include the main ideas and most significant details, use the student's own words, and reflect underlying meaning

After You Read

Retell It!

Work with a partner. Retell the story as an interview. One of you will be the reporter and the other will be Emma Garcia. Be sure to include all of the important events and facts from the reading passage. Tape your interview.

Think, Discuss, Write

Discuss these questions in small groups. Write your answers on a separate sheet of paper.

1. **Point of view**   Who is the narrator of this article? What is the point of view?

2. **Recall details**   What is the first youth violence-prevention program in the U.S.?

3. **Recall details**   What four areas of violence did the 1989 fall conference cover?

4. **Make inferences**   Why did Emma urge lawmakers to ban billboards that advertise liquor and cigarettes?

5. **Theme**   What was the important theme of Emma's message that she brought to the national conference for public officials?

6. **Structure**   The article about Emma Garcia is a nonfiction narrative. What are some of the characteristics of this form of writing?

7. **Compare and contrast**   Compare the excerpt from "The Last Princess" with the article about Emma Garcia. How are they similar? How are they different in content and structure?

Reading: Identify structural patterns found in informational text to strengthen comprehension

What's Your Opinion?

Work with a partner. Compare Emma with Princess Ka'iulani. Both demonstrate courage, but in different ways. Create a diagram like the one shown to indicate what they have in common and how they are different.

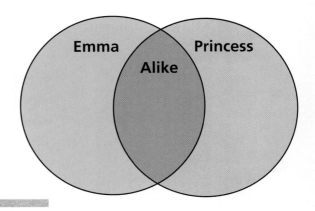

Launch into Grammar

Subjects and verbs   A complete sentence must have a subject and verb (predicate). The **subject** is the word (or words) that explains who or what the sentence is about. The **verb** is the word (or words) that explains the action of the sentence. Subjects and verbs should always agree. Singular subjects need singular verbs. Plural subjects need plural verbs.

> Emma learns English in the first grade.
> (singular subject: *Emma*, singular verb: *learns*)

> Emma and her friends write a survey.
> (plural subject: *Emma and her friends*, plural verb: *write*)

With a partner, on a separate sheet of paper, write the form of the verb in parentheses to complete each sentence.

1. Kids (say, says) they desperately want to talk.

2. Emma (receive, receives) training from Youth Alive.

3. Young people (need, needs) more information.

 For more practice with sentence structure, complete page 43 of the Student Workbook.

Written Conventions: Identify types and structure of sentences; Written Conventions: Identify and use subjects and verbs correctly in speaking and writing simple sentences

Mexican dancers at a fiesta.

Launch into Word Analysis

Suffixes   A **suffix** is a word part that attaches to a word root and creates a new word. Suffixes always come *after* the word root. Suffixes can help you figure out the meaning of new words. The suffix *er* means *someone who* or *more.* In the story, several words using the *er* suffix are used.

Example: teacher = someone who teaches

On a separate sheet of paper, write the following words and their meanings.

workers   voters   dealers

 For more practice with suffixes, complete page 44 in the Student Workbook.

Reading: Use knowledge of Greek, Latin, and Anglo-Saxon roots and affixes to understand content-area vocabulary;
Reading: Read common word families

Launch into Writing

Supporting facts Any statements, or conclusions, or opinions you voice in your own writing should be backed up by supporting facts. Supporting facts include details, examples, and other forms of information for your position. In the example below, the underlined sentences support the paragraph's main idea.

As a result of the conference, Emma Garcia took it upon herself to educate students. <u>She received training from Youth Alive, a public health agency.</u> <u>With her teachers' permission, she gave presentations in junior-high and high-school classes three to four times over a three-week period.</u>

With a partner, write your own paragraph on a separate sheet of paper. Start with a clear main idea. Then provide supporting facts that back up the main idea. Underline each supporting fact. Work with a partner.

 For more practice with supporting facts, use pages 46–47 of the Student Workbook.

Writing Tip

Before you begin to write, think about your audience. Who will read your work?

The way in which you write, the vocabulary that you use, and most of all, what you write about should be appropriate for your readers.

Reading: Distinguish facts, supported inferences, and opinions in text

7

Call It Courage

an excerpt from a novel
by Armstrong Sperry

Before You Read

Background

It takes a special kind of courage to face your greatest fears. In the excerpt from *Call It Courage,* you will read about Mafatu, a boy who is terrified of the sea. Since all boys and men on Hikueru island are expected to fish, Mafatu's fear of the ocean makes his life extremely difficult. Determined to make a new start in a place where he will not be known as a coward, he sets off on a dangerous adventure, and proves himself to be worthy of his name, Stout Heart. Have you ever had to overcome a big fear?

LEARNING OBJECTIVES

- Identify themes across sources
- Learn to use semicolons
- Learn how to recognize word roots
- Learn how to make an outline

Building Your Vocabulary

1. With a partner, read the following words and phrases that have to do with fishing, boats, and the sea. Look up any words you do not know in a dictionary. Add them to your Vocabulary Log.

reef	outrigger canoe
paddle	frigate
bow	swells
bonitos	spear
shaft	lagoon

Reading: Use a dictionary to learn the meaning and other features of unknown words

2. On a poster draw a picture that shows Mafatu's island. Use as many of these words as possible. Label them.

Islanders paddling outrigger canoes.

Reading Strategy

Identify recurring themes The **theme** is the "big" or important message communicated in a story. On the surface, a story may be about a single topic, such as fishing. But deeper down, the story will address bigger issues, or themes, such as courage, friendship, or community.

Applying the Reading Strategy

1. As you read the story, make sure that you completely understand the story's plot and the main ideas.

2. After you finish reading, think about the larger message, or theme. Focus on big issues, such as courage or friendship. Which theme does the story focus on?

3. Think back to other stories you have read in this unit. What major themes did they have? How does the use of this theme compare in all three stories?

4. Apply this strategy to any story you read. As you read, try to understand the story. Then find the story's theme. Finally, try to connect the theme to your own experiences.

Reading: Discern main ideas and concepts presented in texts, identifying and assessing evidence that supports those ideas

Call It Courage

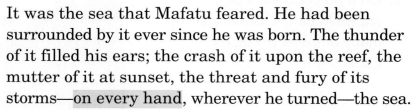

an excerpt from a novel by Armstrong Sperry

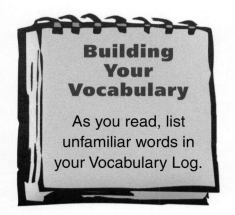

It was the sea that Mafatu feared. He had been surrounded by it ever since he was born. The thunder of it filled his ears; the crash of it upon the reef, the mutter of it at sunset, the threat and fury of its storms—on every hand, wherever he turned—the sea.

He could not remember when the fear of it first had taken hold of him. Perhaps it was during the great hurricane which swept Hikueru when he was a child of three. Even now, twelve years later, Mafatu could remember that terrible morning. His mother had taken him out to the barrier-reef to search for sea urchins in the reef pools. There were other canoes scattered at wide intervals along the reef. With late afternoon the other fishermen began to turn back. They shouted warnings to Mafatu's mother. It was the season of hurricanes and the people of Hikueru were nervous and ill at ease, charged, it seemed, with an almost animal awareness of impending storm.

But when at last Mafatu's mother turned back toward shore, a swift current had set in around the shoulder of the reef-passage: a meeting of tides that swept like a millrace out into the open sea. It seized the frail craft in its swift race. Despite all the woman's skill, the canoe was carried on the crest of the churning tide, through the reef-passage, into the outer ocean.

Mafatu would never forget the sound of his mother's despairing cry. He didn't know then what

on every hand: all over; everywhere
millrace: a strong current of water

Reading: Discern main ideas and concepts presented in texts, identifying and assessing evidence that supports those ideas

it meant; but he felt that something was terribly wrong, and he set up a loud wailing. Night closed down upon them, swift as a frigate's wing, darkening the known world. The wind of the open ocean rushed in at them, screaming. Waves lifted and struck at one another, their crests hissing with spray. The poles of the outrigger were torn from their thwarts. The woman sprang forward to seize her child as the canoe capsized. The little boy gasped when the cold water struck him. He clung to his mother's neck. Moana, the Sea God, was reaching up for them, seeking to draw them down to his dark heart . . . .

Off the tip of Hikueru, the uninhabited islet of Tekoto lay shrouded in darkness. It was scarcely more than a ledge of coral, almost awash. The swift current bore directly down upon the islet.

Dawn found the woman still clinging to the purau pole and the little boy with his arms locked about his mother's neck. The grim light revealed sharks circling, circling. . . . Little Mafatu buried his head against his mother's cold neck. He was filled with terror. He even forgot the thirst that burned his throat. But the palms of Tekoto beckoned with their promise of life, and the woman fought on.

When at last they were cast up on the pinnacle of coral, Mafatu's mother crawled ashore

thwart: a seat in the canoe
purau: canoe pole
pinnacle: the highest point

As You Read

1. How old is he now?
2. What do you think is the meaning of *islet* in "the uninhabited islet of Tekoto"?

Call It Courage 79

with scarcely enough strength left to pull her child beyond reach of the sea's hungry fingers. The little boy was too weak even to cry. At hand lay a cracked coconut; the woman managed to press the cool, sustaining meat to her child's lips before she died.

Sometimes now, in the hush of night, when the moon was full and its light lay in silver bands across the pandanus mats, and all the village was sleeping, Mafatu awoke and sat upright. The sea muttered its eternal threat to the reef. The sea . . . . And a terrible trembling seized the boy's limbs, while a cold sweat broke out on his forehead. Mafatu seemed to see again the faces of the fishermen who had found the dead mother and her whimpering child. These pictures still colored his dreams. And so it was that he shuddered when the mighty seas, gathering far out, hurled themselves at the barrier-reef of Hikueru and the whole island quivered under the assault.

Perhaps that was the beginning of it. Mafatu, the boy who had been christened Stout Heart by his proud father, was afraid of the sea. What manner of fisherman would he grow up to be? How would he ever lead the men in battle against warriors of other islands? Mafatu's father heard the whispers, and the man grew silent and grim.

The older people were not unkind to the boy, for they believed that it was all the fault of the tupapau—the ghost-spirit which possesses every child at birth. But the girls laughed at him, and

pandanus: pine leaves woven together

As You Read

1. Why is Mafatu's father silent and grim?
2. What is the tupapau?

Reading: Discern main ideas and concepts presented in texts, identifying and assessing evidence that supports those ideas

the boys failed to include him in their games. And the voice of the reef seemed pitched for his ears alone; it seemed to say: "You cheated me once, Mafatu, but someday, someday I will claim you!"

Mafatu's stepmother knew small sympathy for him, and his stepbrothers treated him with open scorn.

"Listen," they would mock. "Moana, the Sea God, thunders on the reef. He is angry with us all because Mafatu is afraid!"

The boy learned to turn these jibes aside, but his father's silence shamed him. He tried with all his might to overcome his terror of the sea. Sometimes, steeling himself against it, he went with Tavana Nui and his stepbrothers out beyond the reef to fish. Out there, where the glassy swells of the ocean lifted and dropped the small canoe, pictures crowded into the boy's mind, setting his scalp atingle: pictures of himself, a babe, clinging to his mother's back . . . sharks cruising. . . . And so overcome would he be at the remembrance of that time that he would drop his spear overboard, or let the line go slack at the wrong moment and lose the fish.

It was obvious to everyone that Mafatu was useless upon the sea. He would never earn his proper place in the tribe. Stout Heart—how bitter the name must taste upon his father's lips!

So, finally, he was not allowed to fare forth with the fisherman. He brought ill luck. He had

small: little

open scorn: no respect

setting: causing

scalp atingle: a prickly feeling on your scalp

As You Read

1. Who is Moana?
2. Why do the boys think Mafatu will never be a warrior?

Call It Courage   81

to stay at home making spears and nets, twisting coir—the husk of the coconut—into stout sharkline for other boys to use. He became very skillful at these pursuits, but he hated them. His heart was like a stone in his breast.

A nondescript yellow dog named Uri was Mafatu's inseparable companion—Uri with his thin coat which showed his ribs, and his eyes so puzzled and true. He followed the boy wherever he went. Their only other friend was Kivi, an albatross. The boy had once found the bird on his lonely wanderings. One of Kivi's feet was smaller than the other. Perhaps because it was different from its kind, the older birds were heckling and pestering the fledgling. Something about that small bird trying to fight off its more powerful fellows touched the boy's heart. He picked it up and carried it home—caught fish for it in the shallows of the lagoon. The bird followed Mafatu and Uri about, limping on its one good leg. At length, when the young albatross learned to fly, it began to find its own food. In the air it achieved perfection, floating serenely against the sky while Mafatu followed its effortless flight with envious eyes. If only he, too, could escape to some world far removed from Hikueru!

Now, once more, it was the beginning of the season of storms. Men scanned the skies anxiously, watching for the dreaded signs which might spell the destruction of their world. Soon the great bonitos

nondescript: ordinary-looking
fledgling: a young bird who does not fly yet

Reading: Discern main ideas and concepts presented in texts, identifying and assessing evidence that supports those ideas

would be swimming beyond the reef—hundreds, thousands of them—for they came each year at this time with the unfailing regularity of the tides. They were held to be the special property of young boys, since it was by killing them that a youth learned to kill the swordfishes and tiger-sharks, progressing from one stage to a higher stage. Every boy in the village sharpened his spear, tested the shaft, honed his shark knife. Every boy, that is, except Mafatu.

His hands were damp and cold. His nails dug into his palms. Suddenly a fierce resentment stormed through him. He knew in that instant what he must do: he must prove his courage to himself, and to the others, or he could no longer live in their midst. He must face Moana, the Sea God—face him and conquer him. He must.

The boy stood there taut as a drawn arrow awaiting its release. Off to the south somewhere there were other islands. . . . He drew a deep breath. If he could win his way to a distant island, he could make a place for himself among strangers. And he would never return to Hikueru until he should have proven himself! He would come back with his head high—held in pride—and he would hear his father say: "Here is my son Stout Heart. A brave name for a brave boy." . . . Standing there with clenched fists, Mafatu knew a smarting on his eyelids and shut his eyes tight, and sank his teeth into his lower lip.

Far off in the himené house the Old Ones were singing. Their voices filled the night with rich sound.

property: possessions
himené: the house where the people of the island sing

As You Read

1. What does Mafatu want to prove to himself and others?

2. What are the themes of the Old Ones' songs?

Call It Courage 83

They sang of long voyages in open canoes, of hunger and thirst and battle. They sang the deeds of heroes. The hair on the boy's damp forehead stirred; the long—drawn mutter of the reef sounded its note of warning in his ears. At his side, Uri touched his master's hand with a cold nose. Mafatu pulled the dog close.

"We're going away, Uri," he whispered fiercely. "Off to the south there are other islands." . . .

The outrigger canoes lay drawn up on the beach like long slim fish. Silent as a shadow, the boy crossed the sand. His heart was hammering in his throat. Into the nearest canoe he flung half a dozen green drinking nuts, his fish spear. He gave his pareu a brave hitch. Then he picked up a paddle and called to Uri. The dog leaped into the bow. There was only Kivi—Mafatu would miss his albatross. He scanned the dark sky for sight of the bird, then gave it up and turned away.

The lagoon was as untroubled as a mirror. Upon its black face the stars lay tracks of fire. The boy shoved off and climbed into the stern. Noiselessly he propelled the canoe forward, sending it half a length ahead with each thrust of his paddle. As he drew nearer to the barrier-reef, the thunder of the surf increased. The old, familiar dread of it struck at his stomach's pit, and made him falter in his paddling. The voices of the Old Ones were fainter and fainter now.

The reef thunder mounted: a long-drawn, hushed yet mighty sound that seemed to have its being not in the air above but in the very sea

pareu: the cloth skirt worn by people of the island

As You Read

1. What do you think the phrase "his heart was hammering in his throat" means?

2. How does the author describe the sounds of the reef?

Reading: Discern main ideas and concepts presented in texts, identifying and assessing evidence that supports those ideas

beneath. Out beyond lurked a terrifying world of water and wind. Out there lay everything most to be feared. The boy's hands tightened on his paddle. Behind him lay safety, security from the sea. What matter if they jeered? For a second he almost turned back. Then he heard Kana's voice once more saying: "Mafatu is a coward."

The canoe entered the race formed by the ebbing tide. It caught up the small craft in its churn, swept it forward like a chip on a millrace. No turning back now. . . .

The boy was aware of a sudden whir and fury in the sky above, the beat of mighty wings. Startled, he glanced upward. There was Kivi, his albatross. Mafatu's heart lifted. The bird circled slowly in the moonlight, its wings edged with silver. It hovered for a moment just over the bow of the canoe, then it rose easily, lightly in its effortless flight. Out through the passage in the reef. Out into the open ocean.

Mafatu gripped the steering paddle and followed.

churn: violent waves

As You Read

1. Why does Mafatu's heart lift?

2. What happens to Mafatu after Kivi arrives?

3. How many times does the author use the word *out* in the material on page 85? What does this repetition do?

About the Author
Armstrong Sperry (1897–1976)

Armstrong Sperry was born in New Haven, Connecticut. Educated at Yale School of Fine Art, he served in the United States Navy and worked as a commercial artist and illustrator.

Reading: Discern main ideas and concepts presented in texts, identifying and assessing evidence that supports those ideas

After You Read

Retell It!

Work in a small group. Retell the story using as many adjectives of sound, smell, and feelings as you can.

Think, Discuss, Write

In small groups, discuss these questions. Write your answers on a separate sheet of paper.

1. **Setting**   Describe the different settings of the story. How many can you identify?

2. **Cause and effect**   Why is Mafatu afraid of the sea?

3. **Recall details**   What name did Mafatu's father give him at birth?

4. **Recall details**   Why is Mafatu not allowed to go with the fishermen?

5. **Make inferences**   Why were Uri and Kivi so important to Mafatu?

6. **Predict**   In your opinion, what happens to Mafatu after he follows Kivi?

7. **Compare and contrast** What words are used to contrast the safety of land with the danger of the sea?

What's Your Opinion?

Work with a partner. Make a list of five characteristics of a courageous person. Then rank them on a Ranking Ladder

Ranking Ladder:
Most Important
courage
Least Important

Reading: Extract appropriate and significant information from the text, including problems and solutions

like the one shown, with the least important at the bottom of the ladder and the most important at the top of the ladder. Share your ladder with the rest of the class. Do you agree with your classmates' charts?

Launch into Grammar

Semicolons Independent clauses are clauses that can stand by themselves as sentences. You can join two independent clauses in two different ways: using a *conjunction (and, but, or, for)* or a *semicolon.*

> The girls laughed at him, and the boys failed to include him. (conjunction: *and)*

> The girls laughed at him; the boys failed to include him. (semicolon)

Note that in the second sentence, the semicolon simply replaced the conjunction and the comma.

Rewrite each sentence using a semicolon. Work on a separate sheet of paper.

1. Mafatu was afraid, but he had learned to overcome his fear.

2. He knew he needed to leave, and he needed to leave soon.

3. The bonitos would come, but Mafatu would not catch any of them.

 For more practice with punctuation, use page 51 of the Student Workbook.

History

A thousand years before Christopher Columbus sailed from Europe, Polynesian sailors crossed thousands of miles of ocean. They were guided only by their observations of nature. They watched the sun during the day and the moon and stars at night. Even though they had no navigational instruments, they knew how to find the way to Hawai'i and other specific locations in the Pacific Ocean.

Call It Courage 87

Written Conventions: Identify semicolons and use them correctly; Written Conventions: Use semicolons to connect independent clauses

Launch into Word Analysis

Word roots   Many words stem from the same *word root.* Prefixes, suffixes, and other additions change the root's meaning. You can figure out the meaning of new words if you know the meaning of their root. In *Call It Courage,* you will find the words *terrible, terror, terrifying,* and *terribly.* Each of these words has the same root, *terr,* which means "striking fear."

The story also has the word *courage,* which is based on a root word *cour,* which means "heart." Write the following words on a sheet of paper. With a partner, find the definition for each one. Can you see how these relate to "heart"? How do the prefixes and suffixes change the meaning?

courage	discourage
encourage	courageous

For more practice with word roots, use page 52 of the Student Workbook.

Reading: Know common roots and affixes derived from Greek and Latin and use this knowledge to analyze the meaning of complex words

Launch into Writing

Writing Tip

Write a topic sentence for each of your paragraphs. A **topic sentence** gives the main idea of your paragraph. It gives your readers an idea of what the paragraph will be about and it should catch their interest.

Write an outline   An **outline** is a way to organize important facts and details in order. You can use one to write a first draft.

Read an article about the South Seas or some other tropical destination in an encyclopedia or on the Internet. Take notes on the article using the strategy of outlining. Follow this format to complete your outline.

Example: South Seas

       I.   Location
            A.
            B.
     II.   Climate
            A.
            B.
   III.   People
            A.
            B.

For more practice outlining, use pages 54–55 of the workbook.

Writing: Use various reference materials (dictionary, online information) as an aid to writing

8

She's Wearing
a
Dead Bird
on Her Head!

**a story
by Kathryn Lasky**

Background

When Harriet Hemenway realized that birds were being slaughtered so that women could wear them as decorations on their hats, she was horrified. Although women had very little power in 1896, she and her cousin, Minna, were determined to put an end to this deadly fashion trend. In this selection, you will read about the courage and efforts of a small group of dedicated individuals who truly made a difference.

Do you think we should protect animals more than we do today?

LEARNING OBJECTIVES

- Identify an author's point of view
- Learn to recognize an infinitive
- Learn to recognize contractions
- Learn to prepare a counterargument

Building Your Vocabulary

1. Harriet and Minna use a variety of bird names. Here are some of them:

   egrets   warblers
   pheasants   marabou

2. Work with a partner. Use your dictionary, your school library, or your computer to research these different types of birds. Try to find pictures of the

Reading: Use a dictionary to find the meaning of unknown words.

birds. Have you ever seen one of these birds? On a separate sheet of paper, write one sentence about each bird. Add these bird names to your Vocabulary Log. Share your sentences in a small group or with your class.

Reading Strategy

Identify an author's point of view   Some kinds of writing allow an author to express an opinion or attitude. As a reader, your first job is to discover what the author's position on the topic is. Second, find the reasons behind the author's point of view. Finally, decide how you feel about the topic.

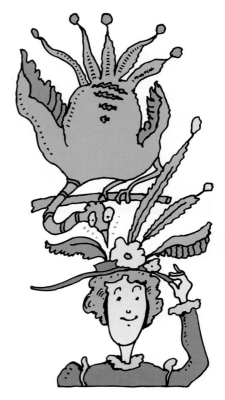

Applying the Reading Strategy

1. Read the story carefully. Note that it is historical fiction — the story relates true events in a fictional form. Look for clues that the author holds an opinion on a topic and wishes to express this opinion. For example, pay attention to sentences that begin with *I think, In my opinion,* or *I feel.*

2. Once you determine the author's opinion, look for evidence and reasoning to support this opinion. Look for facts, details, data, examples, and logical arguments to back up the author's point of view.

3. Make a judgment about the case that the author presents. Does the author's position make sense? Does it seem well argued? Does the evidence seem convincing? Decide how you feel about the position or issue.

4. Use this same approach whenever you come across writing that has an opinion. Keep in mind that authors can state opinions in stories like this one, as well as in essays, editorials, and other non-story formats.

She's Wearing a Dead Bird on Her Head!   91

She's Wearing a Dead Bird on Her Head!

a story by Kathryn Lasky

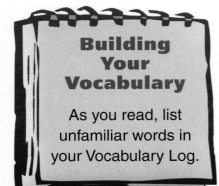

Harriet Hemenway was a very proper Boston lady—she never talked with her mouth full. But one day she almost did. Standing by the bay window in her parlor, she had just bitten into a jam cookie when her eyes sprang open in dismay. She gasped, leaned forward, swallowed, then turned to her parlor maid.

"She's wearing a dead bird on her head!"

Feathers on ladies' hats were becoming more and more popular. At first, hats had been decorated with just feathers, and then designers began to add pairs of wings. But this woman had an entire bird perched atop her hat! Harriet squinted her eyes as the lady of fashion walked proudly by.

"Arctic tern, I believe," Harriet whispered.

"Looks ready to fly away," said the parlor maid.

"It won't," Harriet replied sadly.

Harriet felt that she had to do something. Huge populations of birds, from egrets to pheasants to owls to warblers, were being slaughtered for hat decoration—none were spared. Not even pigeons! But what could she do? Women in 1896 had very little power. They could not vote, and many had husbands who did not allow them to make decisions for themselves. Some women were not even allowed to read newspapers! Harriet's husband, Augustus, did not treat her this way.

But she and other women like her wanted to change things for all women. And she wanted to do something for the birds. Fashion was killing birds

Reading: Use knowledge of the author's purpose to comprehend text

as well as killing women's chances to have the right to vote and be listened to. For who would listen to a woman with a dead bird on her head? And if the senseless slaughter for a silly fashion was not stopped, in a few years the birds with the prettiest feathers would all be dead, gone forever, extinct.

"I must call cousin Minna," Harriet said grimly.

When Minna stormed into the parlor, Harriet was preparing tea.

"Well, Harriet," Minna exclaimed as she pulled off her felt cap. "From Arlington Street to Clarendon—three egrets, one marabou, two grebes, one golden finch, and. . ." Minna paused. Her cousin waited nervously, the teacup chattering on the saucer she was holding. "A hummingbird!"

"Oh no, Minna!"

"Oh yes, Harriet—perched in full flight on a bunch of silk roses with a veil."

"Disgusting!"

"Revolting!"

"Nauseating!"

"Vile!"

The words flew through the air like red-hot cinders.

"Dear, dear. . ." Minna moaned and sipped the last of her tea. "What shall we do?"

"Well." Harriet scratched her head. "We have garden clubs and history clubs—why not form a bird club! Not to just watch birds, no, but to protect them and stop this senseless murdering for fashion."

cinders: fragments of ash or something that has been burned

Reading: Use knowledge of the author's purpose to comprehend text

"What a wonderful idea," said Minna. "Let's do it. Let's start a club for the birds."

Right then they began to write letters to all the Boston ladies of fashion who wore the plumage of birds, imploring them to put aside their fancy hats with swirls of owl feathers, breasts of grebes, wings of hummingbirds, and plumes of egrets and instead join a society dedicated to protecting all birds. This was the first informal meeting of the Audubon Society, named after a man they admired, John Audubon, the famous painter of birds.

Harriet and Minna were very persuasive. They convinced women not only that killing birds was wrong but that birds as hat decoration made women look silly. Soon many of the fashionable ladies of Boston to whom they had written letters did join the society.

For the club to accomplish its goals, however, Harriet and Minna knew it also needed men— smart, powerful men who could vote and go into public places like the state legislatures and the halls of Congress in Washington, D.C. So they asked lawyers and doctors, sportsmen, and bird experts to join, too.

At the second meeting of the Audubon Society, Harriet and Minna and the new members made up rules for their club.

"I think," said one gentleman, "that there should be an exception made for ducks."

"What kind of exception?" Harriet asked.

plumage: the feathers of a bird

Reading: Use knowledge of the author's purpose to comprehend text

"We want to hunt them," replied another gentleman.

"Rules are rules," fumed Minna.

"Sportsmen aren't special," another woman said, and stamped her foot.

The women won. There would be no killing of ducks or game birds. Then all the members devised a plan to get the word out on birds to everyone. And the Bird Hat Campaign of the Audubon Society began in earnest.

They decided to bring their cause to the children of the state of Massachusetts. So into the schools they went—Minna, Harriet, and other members of the society.

"In Florida, heaps of birds, stripped of their feathers, are left dying on the ground," Harriet told one class of children, holding up a photograph of a pile of dead egrets.

"What happened to their babies, the ones left in the nest?" a student asked.

"The ones that are too young to fly are left to die. So you see, we need your help, the *birds* need your help, to protect them against the plume hunters and the hatmakers. Please join our club."

Soon there were over ten thousand junior members of the Audubon Society in the state of Massachusetts. And Audubon societies were formed in other states. More children joined.

The membership in Boston continued to grow, and the meetings were always lively.

"The orange groves in Florida this year are suffering because there are too many dead

As You Read

1. Who is the club named for?

2. Why do Harriet and Minna name their club after a painter of birds?

in earnest: very seriously

groves: a group of trees

Reading: Use knowledge of the author's purpose to comprehend text

hummingbirds on hats and not enough in the groves eating the pests that spoil the fruit," said Miss Harriet Richards, the secretary of the society.

"Let's get the farmers on our side. Send out a letter!" Minna said.

In the club everybody was equal. The women and the men of the society wrote up their ideas together and then sent the gentlemen to talk to legislators in the State House and to members of Congress in Washington, D.C., to press for the passage of laws to save the birds. They were successful! An act was passed in 1903 to protect herons and bitterns, two popular hat birds, from hatmakers, forbidding them to sell, display, or possess the feathers. In 1904 there was another victory when a law was passed to protect shore, marsh, and beach birds.

Soon there were laws against hunting birds during their breeding seasons. And then a federal law was passed preventing the importation of feathers from Europe and the tropics for hats. The word about birds had spread all the way to England, where Queen Victoria had announced that she would never again wear a feather for fashion.

But Minna and Harriet were still far from happy.

"What good is a law if it isn't enforced," Minna moaned one day as she stood looking out the window at a woman passing by with a pheasant's

marsh: low-lying, wet land

As You Read

1. How does killing birds affect the orange groves in Florida?

2. Which two birds are protected by the act passed in 1903?

3. How are birds protected by the additional laws that were passed?

4. Why do the two ladies buy the hats in New York?

Reading: Use knowledge of the author's purpose to comprehend text

wing taking the air above her. "You can't arrest the lady for wearing the hat."

"But you can arrest the supplier of the feather," Harriet said. She tapped her head lightly as if to give a little jostle to her brains. "There are rumors about secret feather warehouses." She spoke softly. "I think we should make a few inquiries."

So the two ladies, with Harriet's husband, Augustus, took the train to New York City, where they were not so well known. They got as gussied up as two Boston ladies who loved birds and hated fashion could manage. They sashayed down Fifth Avenue in fancy dresses and wore elaborate hats with streamers and ribbons— but no feathers! Into the fanciest hat store the two cousins and Augustus Hemenway pranced.

"I want to buy my wife and dear cousin each a hat, a feathered hat," Augustus announced.

The salespeople began fluttering around the prosperous-looking threesome.

"What will it be, madams? Egrets or doves? A dear little cloche covered with owl feathers or this broad-brimmed hat with the

gussied: dressed up

sashayed: walked around proudly, especially to be noticed

cloche: a woman's hat

arctic tern? Is it not spectacular on the blue felt, just as if it is plunging into the sea?"

The two ladies swallowed their disgust and muffled their anger. After all, there were more important things at stake.

By the end of the shopping expedition they, alas, had to buy two hats, but they also had the name of the feather supplier with a warehouse in Baltimore where millions of dead birds and tons of plumes were stored. With this information they went directly to the authorities.

Soon after, on a rainy May day, the cousins sat sipping tea. Harriet had just bitten into a crisp wafer when like a tidal wave Augustus burst into the parlor.

"Ladies!" He held a newspaper aloft in his hand. "You've won!"

"We what?" said Minna. She and Harriet held their breath.

"Won, dear cousin and dear wife! Twenty-six thousand illegal gull skins destined for hats of fashion were seized last night from the Baltimore warehouse. They have shut it down, taken the skins, and arrested the owner." Augustus paused. His rain-slicked face beamed with pride. "The law has been enforced!"

Minna looked at her cousin. "Harriet, we won!"

But Harriet said nothing—for Harriet Hemenway never spoke with her mouth full, even when she won.

at stake: to consider or worry about

As You Read

1. After the women go shopping, where do they go? Why?

2. Why does Augustus say "You've won!"?

Reading: Use knowledge of the author's purpose to comprehend text

John James Audubon (1785–1851) studied art in France with the great French neoclassical painter Jacques-Louis David. His love of birds led him to the decision to make painting them his life's work. He traveled across America collecting and drawing birds. When he realized that there was not very much interest in his project in the United States, he moved to England. His book, *The Birds of America*, was finished in 1838. For this book, he painted 435 life-size paintings of 1,065 birds.

About the Author

Kathryn Lasky

Kathryn Lasky has written over fifty fiction and nonfiction books. She has won many awards including a Newbery Honor for her book *Sugar Time*. *She's Wearing a Dead Bird on Her Head!* is only one of Lasky's historical novels. She also has written about the Salem witch trials (*Beyond the Burning Time*), and the Underground Railroad (*True North*).

She's Wearing a Dead Bird on Her Head! 99

Retell It!

With a partner, retell the story as a front page news article. Tell who is involved, what they are upset about, and what they want people to do about it.

Think, Discuss, Write

Work with a partner. Write your answers on a separate sheet of paper.

1. **Structure**   Is this story fiction or nonfiction? What clues in the story tell you?

2. **Structure**   From what point of view is the story told?

3. **Recall details**   Name two things women were not allowed to do in the 1890s.

4. **Make inferences**   How did Harriet and Minna change the way we think about birds today?

5. **Recall details**   Why did Harriet and Minna ask powerful men to join the club?

6. **Cause and effect**   Why was it important that the feather supplier warehouse was shut down?

7. **Connecting themes**   Emma Garcia and Harriet Hemenway both started clubs to achieve their goals. Discuss how attitudes toward girls and women in the two different eras made a difference in how they went about promoting their programs.

Reading: Demonstrate comprehension by identifying answers in the text

What's Your Opinion?

Kathryn Lasky uses different techniques to make her main points. With a partner, rate the effectiveness of each point on a Ranking Ladder.

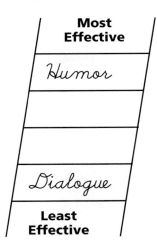

Most Effective

Humor

Dialogue

Least Effective

Launch into Grammar

Infinitives   An **infinitive** is made up of a verb plus the preposition *to.* Examples of infinitive phrases include *to run, to eat,* and *to play.* Infinitives can function as a noun, an adjective, or an adverb.

> **Noun:** She wanted *to stop* the needless slaughter of birds.
> *(to stop* is a direct object)
>
> **Noun:** *To kill* birds is wrong.
> *(to kill* is the subject)
>
> **Adjective:** Harriet had a way *to end* the killing.
> *(to end* modifies *way)*
>
> **Adverb:** She was happy *to find* support.
> *(to find* modifies *happy)*

Find other examples of infinitives in this chapter and write them on a separate sheet of paper. Does each work as a noun, an adjective, or an adverb?

 For more practice with infinitives, complete page 59 of the Student Workbook.

Written Conventions: Identify and use infinitives; Written Conventions: Identify and correctly use various parts of speech in writing and speaking

Launch into Word Analysis

Contractions   A **contraction** combines two words into one shorter word using an apostrophe. Here are some examples:

> could + not → couldn't
>
> they + will → they'll
>
> I + am → I'm

The apostrophe in the contraction takes the place of the letters that are missing in the combined word. The words *you* and *would* combine to form *you'd.* The apostrophe takes the place of the missing letters *woul.*

With a partner, on a separate sheet of paper, identify the contraction in each sentence below. Write the two words that the contraction is made of.

1. She's wearing a dead bird on her head!

2. Let's start a club for the birds.

3. "Sportsmen aren't special," another woman said.

4. "What good is a law if it isn't enforced?" Minna moaned.

 For more practice with contractions, use page 60 of the Student Workbook.

Written Conventions: Use apostrophes in contractions

Launch into Writing

Counterarguments To effectively state your position in writing, you should address any counterarguments that your readers might have. A **counterargument** is a position that goes against your own opinion. To get readers to take you seriously, you need to show that your argument can answer any important questions or concerns that your readers might have.

With a partner, write a counterargument for each of the following positions—even if you agree with the position—on a separate sheet of paper.

1. Birds should not be killed so they can be displayed as decorations.

2. It's okay to kill animals for food but not for fur.

3. Anyone who eats meat should not complain about killing animals.

 For more practice with counterarguments, use pages 62–63 of the Student Workbook.

Writing: Write persuasive compositions: State a clear position, support the position with evidence, and anticipate and address reader concerns and counterarguments

Panel Discussion: Persuade Others

It takes courage to take a stand. Work in groups of four. You will be one of three experts on a television talk show. You'll need a moderator, too. You will identify a problem and take a stand. You will try to convince your audience to agree with you.

Step One: Plan Your Panel Discussion

1. What will you take a stand on? Here are some ideas: leash laws for dogs, rules against riding scooters on sidewalks, bicycle helmet laws, seatbelt laws, or year-round schools.

2. After choosing a topic, research that topic. Go to the library, or look up information on the Internet. Note details that support your position.

3. As a group, make a list of questions for the moderator to ask. Some should challenge the experts' position.

4. Experts should support their stand and prepare answers to the moderator's questions. The moderator should ask questions that challenge the position taken by the experts.

5. Use gestures, facial expressions, and tone of voice to convince your audience.

6. What graphs, tables, charts, or illustrations can you use to support your position? Consider adding these visuals to add impact.

Step Two: Practice Your Panel Discussion

1. Practice presenting your panel discussion. Moderators practice asking questions and experts practice answering them.

2. Use the Speaking Checklist to help you prepare your presentation.

3. Record or videotape your panel discussion. Watch or listen to it. How can you improve?

Writing: Create information reports: Frame a central question about an issue, include facts and details for focus, and draw from more than one source of information

Step Three:
Present Your Panel Discussion

Present your panel discussion. Be ready to invite any students who have opinions to express them briefly during your presentation.

Step Four:
Evaluate Your Panel Discussion

After your panel discussion, ask your audience whether they have any questions or comments. Did they enjoy the panel's comments? Which argument did they find most convincing? Why?

Record Your Panel Discussion

Add a tape of your panel discussion to the classroom listening center. Listen to your own and others' tapes. Check out a tape to share at home with family members.

Speaking Checklist

✔ I used the appropriate tone of voice.

✔ I spoke slowly and clearly.

✔ I used appropriate body language and gestures.

✔ I made eye contact with my audience.

Writing: Create information reports: Frame a central question about an issue, include facts and details for focus, and draw from more than one source of information

Write a Persuasive Composition

Now it's your turn to use the courage of your convictions to take a stand. Write a persuasive composition that convinces your audience to make a change. Do you want your school to add a new club? Do you want the local skate park to stay open longer hours? Include a strong thesis statement, supporting details, and a call to action to make your argument convincing.

Here's an example:

Clean up North Wellington Park

North Wellington Park was once a wonderful place to ride bikes and have fun. However, sadly, things have changed.

North Wellington Park is now dirty and unsafe. Due to community budget cuts, it seems as if there are not enough workers to maintain the park.

If North Wellington Park were cleaned up, this would have a positive effect on the community.

It would be in the best interests of local lawmakers to clean up North Wellington Park. So, get on the phone or write a letter to local lawmakers, and tell them to clean up the park!

Writing: Write persuasive compositions: State a clear position in support of a proposal, support a position with relevant evidence, follow a simple organizational pattern, and address reader concerns

1. Pre-write

Decide on your purpose and audience. Who will your readers be? What will you write about? What examples can you use to convince others? Create a word web to organize your ideas.

2. Draft

Follow these steps to organize your persuasive composition.

A. Get your reader's interest. Start with an opening sentence that you think will get others' attention.

B. State your opinion. Use clear language and summarize your main points.

C. Each paragraph should give a reason to support your position. After each reason, provide details that support it. Try to save your strongest reason for the last paragraph.

D. Conclude with a call to action. Restate your opinion in a way that invites others to agree with you.

3. Revise

A. Have I captured my reader's interest in the opening paragraph?

B. Have I given support for my position?

C. Have I used details to support my position?

Consider your answers to these questions as you revise your persuasive essay.

4. Edit and Proofread

Proofread your revised essay. Check sentence punctuation, capitalization, and spelling. Look in the dictionary to verify spelling of words.

5. Publish

Now you are ready to publish your persuasive composition. Consider using a computer and printing out your composition. Send it to a local newspaper or put it in a class newspaper. Will you put your persuasive compositions on an editorial page? Generally, pieces in which people try to convince others of a position are included on the editorial pages. These pieces give opinions.

Writing: Edit and revise selected drafts to improve coherence and progression by adding, deleting, consolidating, clarifying, and rearranging words and sentences

Community Action

Project Goal

In this unit you read about courage and standing up for your rights. With a partner, create a poster. Ask people to a meeting about a community project.

With a partner, choose a **problem** that affects your neighborhood. Is there a park that needs to be cleaned up? Is there litter? Do sidewalks need to be fixed? Do people need bike paths?

Use the newspaper or Internet to find out what others are doing to try to create **community awareness** of the problem. Make a list of what you can do to **alleviate**, or fix, it. Will you hold a meeting with your neighbors to discuss this problem? Can you have a local police officer or other community official speak about this problem? Who will your main speaker be?

Design a poster to advertise your community meeting. **Persuade** people to come. Tell them how this problem affects your neighborhood. Explain to them how they can solve this problem if they all come together to fix it. Give the date and the time.

Show your poster to the class. Would others in your class like to come to your meeting?

Check Your Progress

Listening/Speaking Did you make a poster to advertise your meeting?
Reading Did you look through newspapers or the Internet to research what others are doing to help make their communities better places to live?
Writing Did you write a convincing message for your poster? Did you provide information? The time? The date? The problems that need to be solved?

Words to Know

problem
community action
alleviate
persuade

Write research reports about important ideas, issues, or events by framing questions, establishing a controlling idea, and developing the topic with simple facts, details, examples, and explanations

Choose one or more of the following books to read. Write down in your Reading Log the books you read and your opinion of each. Ask yourself these questions:

1. Have you ever had to overcome a fear of something?

2. Why is it sometimes difficult to be courageous?

3. Do you agree with Plato's statement "Courage is knowing what not to fear?"

Fiction

The Lighthouse Keeper's Daughter by Arielle North Olson

When a storm makes it impossible for Miranda's father to return to his lighthouse, Miranda, with a little help from her mother, makes sure the lights stay on.

Hatchet by Gary Paulsen

Brian is on his way to visit his father when the pilot of his plane dies of a heart attack. Alone in the Canadian wilderness with nothing but a hatchet, the thirteen-year-old boy must find ways to survive.

Nonfiction

Chief Joseph: Nez Percé Leader by Marian W. Taylor

Part of a series about Native Americans, this book describes the efforts of Chief Joseph to defend his people, the *Nez Percé,* in war and peace.

Starry Messenger by Peter Sis

Sixteenth-century Italian scientist Galileo Galilei was considered great until he announced his discovery that the Earth moved around the Sun. This theory was unacceptable to philosophers and religious leaders of his time.

Reading: Compare and contrast information on the same topic

UNIT 3
Conflict

"There was never
a good war
or bad peace."
—Benjamin Franklin (American
statesman, author, inventor,
printer, and scientist, 1706–1790)

Discuss the Theme
Resolving Conflicts

A conflict can be as small as an argument between two brothers as in "Argument Sticks" or as big as a war as in the tragic "Zlata's Diary." Sometimes fighting seems like the easiest way to end a disagreement, but resolving conflicts without violence should be everyone's goal. "Robin Hood" seeks justice for the poor without the use of force, and in "Class Bully," one brave boy tries a new move on a bully at school.

- What do you know about conflicts?
- How do wars affect people's everyday lives?
- Have you ever been involved in an argument that you could have avoided?

WRITING FOCUS:
Write a Response to Literature

9

Before You Read

Background

Have you ever been picked on by a bully? How did you react? In this poem, a young boy learns how to control his temper in order to avoid conflict with a classmate.

CLASS BULLY

a poem by Nikki Grimes

LEARNING OBJECTIVES

- Recognize repetition in poetry
- Recognize participles
- Recognize cognates
- Learn to respond to poetry

Building Your Vocabulary

What is a **bully?** Use a dictionary to find the meanings of words you don't know. With a partner, look up the words in the list below. Write down their meanings and parts of speech on a chart in your Vocabulary Log.

fume	grab
return	strong
blow	kick

Reading: Use a dictionary to learn the meaning and other features of unknown words

Word	Part of Speech	Definition
kick	*verb*	*to hit someone or something with the foot or feet*

Reading Strategy

Notice repetition in poetry   A poem communicates its message two ways—through its sound and meaning of words. As you read, the words on the page create images, thoughts, and feelings in your mind. Meanwhile, the sounds of the words speak on a different level, creating a musical rhythm in which words and sounds repeat themselves in a pattern that is pleasing to your ear. When you read poetry, try to appreciate both the sound and the meaning of the words in the poem.

Applying the Reading Strategy

1. Read the poem one time for meaning. Then read and listen to the sound and rhythm of the poem.

2. Pay special attention to words, phrases, and sounds that repeat themselves.

3. Look for patterns in the words, sounds, and phrases that repeat. How do these repetitions affect the meaning of the poem?

4. Read the poem a final time. How well do the sound and the meaning of the poem fit together?

Class Bully   113

CLASS BULLY

a poem by Nikki Grimes

A bully
kicks me in the knee
That bully's name
is Tiffany.
I fume
but don't return the blow.
Guys don't hit girls
Blue says, and so
I grab
her wrists 'til she
calms down, while
Laughing
jeering kids stand 'round
and shout "You wimp!" But
they're all wrong.
It's guys
who *don't* hit girls
Who're strong.

As You Read

1. Who is Blue?
2. Did it surprise you that the bully is a girl? Why?
3. Why does Tiffany kick the boy? Does it matter?
4. What do the last three lines mean?

wimp: a weak person

Reading: Read narrative and expository text aloud with fluency and accuracy

About the Author

Nikki Grimes

Nikki Grimes, an author of books and poems for children, was born and raised in New York City. Several of her books have been named Notable Books by the American Library Association.

Reading: Read narrative and expository text aloud with fluency and accuracy

After You Read

Retell It!

With a partner, tell a story about what happens in the poem. Include all of the details.

Think, Discuss, Write

Discuss the following questions in small groups. Write your answers on a separate sheet of paper.

1. **Structure**   In what tense is the poem written? What effect do you think this has?

2. **Tone**   What is the tone of this poem? How does it help you to better understand the poem?

3. **Setting**   Where does this story take place? How do you know?

4. **Recall details**   What is the bully's name?

5. **Recall details**   Blue's name is only mentioned once. How important do you think Blue is in this poem?

6. **Make inferences**   How do you think Tiffany feels when the boy does not fight back?

7. **Cause and effect**   What effect might the boy's actions have on Tiffany and the other kids?

Reading: Restate facts and details in the text to clarify and organize ideas

What's Your Opinion?

Work in a small group. How do you think this poem should be read? Take turns reading the poem, stressing key words.

Launch into Grammar

Participles   A **participle** is a form of a verb that can used as an adjective or as part of a verb. Present participles end in *-ing*. Past participles usually end in *-ed*.

> **Laughing, jeering** kids stand 'round.

> A girl **named** Tiffany is the bully.

> The kids were **shouting**.

In the first sentence, the participles *laughing* and *jeering* are used as adjectives to modify the noun *kids.* In the second sentence, the participle *named* is used as an adjective to modify the noun *girl.* In the third sentence, the participle *shouting* is part of the verb, *were shouting.*

With a partner, rewrite each sentence on a separate sheet of paper and identify the participle. Tell whether it is used as part of a verb or as an adjective.

1. The surprised kids all looked at me.

2. Tiffany was surprised by my action.

3. The confused bully didn't know what to do.

4. Smiling, Tiffany offered to shake my hand.

Connecting to

Visual and Performing Arts

Artists use many different tools and materials in their work. They may work in oil paint, acrylic, pen and ink, pencil, charcoal, or some other element.

Written conventions: Use participles correctly in writing and speaking

 For more practice with participles, complete page 67 of the Student Workbook.

Launch into Word Analysis

Cognates   Some words have similar spellings and meanings in different languages. Work in groups, where at least one person understands Spanish. Figure out the English meanings of words below and write your answers on a separate sheet of paper.

1. I **fume** but don't return the blow.
   In Spanish, *fumar* means to smoke, so *fume* in English might mean:
   a. get angry and "hot"
   b. fun
   c. fire department

2. I don't have much **sympathy** for bullies.
   In Spanish, *simpatico* means nice, so *sympathy* in English might mean:
   a. friend
   b. mean
   c. kindness

3. We had our **annual** picnic in May this year.
   In Spanish, *ano* means year, so *annual* in English might mean:
   a. calendar
   b. yearly
   c. summer

Study Tip

One of the best ways to learn something is to teach it to someone else. Explain what you are studying to someone else. How well does the person understand? You and a friend can take turns teaching each other.

Reading: Use word origins to determine the meaning of unknown words

Launch into Writing

Respond to a poem   Your response to any two poems should never be the same. When you write a response to a poem:

- Be open, honest, and direct. Don't pretend to like a poem. Write what you really think. Tell how the poem connected (or did not connect) to your life.

- Analyze the meaning of the poem. What did it mean to you? How did it make you feel?

- Analyze the poem's sound. What patterns and rhythms are used? How did you like the poem's sound?

- Analyze the images in the poem. Which images caught your eye? What did you like about them?

    Here is an example of a response to a poem.

"Class Bully" made me want to jump up and shout, "Yes!" The image of all the laughing kids shouting "You wimp!" really got to me. I know how that feels. Also, the rhythm of the way words are repeated is musical!

Writing Tip

When you write a story, try to use the present tense and active voice. It makes your story more interesting and exciting. For example, "Tiffany kicks the boy" seems more alive and exciting then "The boy was kicked by Tiffany."

For more practice responding to poetry, use pages 70–71 of the Student Workbook.

Writing: Write responses to literature: Develop an interpretation, organize the interpretation, develop and justify the interpretation with textual evidence

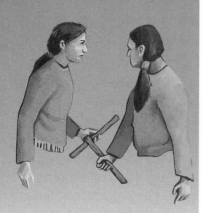

ARGUMENT
STICKS

**an Iroquois folktale
retold by
Margaret Reed
MacDonald**

Background

Different cultures have different ways of settling disagreements. In this short Native American tale, you will see how a wise Iroquois mother teaches her sons to resolve conflict. As you read, make predictions about the outcome of the tale. Why is the mother wise? How do you settle disagreements within your family?

LEARNING OBJECTIVES

- Identify a theme across sources
- Recognize gerunds
- Recognize antonyms
- Identify main ideas in writing

Building Your Vocabulary

1. The following words are used to describe arguments and conflict. With a partner, read them over. Use a dictionary for those terms you do not know.

arguing
wrong
solve
winner
admit
come to blows
right

Reading: Demonstrate knowledge of levels of specificity among grade-appropriate words

2. With a partner, create a ranking ladder like the one shown on a separate sheet of paper. Use the ranking ladder to show which words are the most and least important in resolving conflict.

Most Important
Solve
Right
Least Important

Reading Strategy

Identify themes across sources   When you look at folktales or other kinds of stories, you begin to see themes, or ideas, that repeat themselves. For example, some stories are about truth, or justice, or happiness. Other stories might seem different, but on a deeper level they are exploring the same themes.

Applying the Reading Strategy

1. Read the story carefully. Then identify its theme. Common themes include truth, justice, good and evil, happiness, home, family, and so on.

2. Once you have identified the theme, think back to other stories that have a similar theme. These other stories might be folk tales, poems, novels—even nonfictional stories or historical fiction.

3. Compare the themes of the different sources. What was the same about them? How were they different? What was unique about the theme of this story?

Reading: Connect and clarify main ideas by identifying their relationships to other sources and related topics

ARGUMENT STICKS

an Iroquois folktale retold by Margaret Reed MacDonald

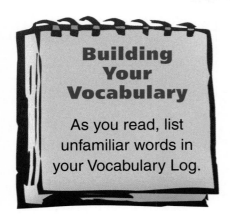

Building Your Vocabulary

As you read, list unfamiliar words in your Vocabulary Log.

As You Read

1. How many sticks do the boys set up?

2. Why do you think this folktale has been passed on from generation to generation?

Two Iroquois boys were arguing.
Neither would admit he was wrong.
They were about to come to blows over this.

Their mother gave them three sticks:
"These are special Argument Sticks.
They will solve this argument for you.
Set your sticks up in the woods,
    leaning one against the other so they all stand up.
Leave them there for one month.
If they fall over toward the north,
    the one who sets up the northern stick
    is right in this matter.
If they fall over toward the south,
    the one who sets up the southern stick
    is right in this matter."

Reading: Connect and clarify main ideas by identifying their relationships to other sources and related topics

The boys took their sticks into the woods and set
them up.
They were satisfied that this would solve their
argument.
A month later the boys remembered their
Argument Sticks.
They went into the woods to find out
who had won the argument.

The sticks had fallen in a heap and
begun to rot. There was no winner.

And the boys couldn't remember
what the argument had been
about in the first place.

Connecting to Mythology

The number **three** appears in the stories, fairy tales, and myths of many different cultures. The Greeks had three Fates, three Muses, three Furies, and three Harpies. The Three Mysterious sat on thrones in Asgard in Scandinavian mythology.

heap: a pile
rot: fall apart and decay

About the Author

This is an Iroquois tale that has been passed down from one generation to another. The Iroquois League was made up of the Mohawk, Onondaga, Cayuga, Oneida, and Seneca, and later the Tuscarora. These Native American nations lived in what is now central New York State. Their economy was mainly agricultural, based on corn, pumpkin, and beans.

Reading: Connect and clarify main ideas by identifying their relationships to other sources and related topics

After You Read

Retell It!

With a partner, retell the story from each brother's point of view. Each of you should take the part of one of the brothers. As one of the brothers, tell what the argument is about and what you learn from the argument sticks.

Think, Discuss, Write

With a partner, write your answers on a separate sheet of paper.

1. **Structure**   Discuss what type of structure "Argument Sticks" has.

2. **Compare and contrast**   This reading is called a tale. How do you think a tale is different from a short story? How is it different from a poem?

3. **Theme**   What is a major theme of this tale?

4. **Recall details**   Who gives the boys the argument sticks?

5. **Point of view**   From whose point of view might this tale be written?

6. **Make inferences**   What do you think the boys might have been arguing about?

7. **Cause and effect**   Do you think the boys' experience with the argument sticks will change the way they deal with conflict?

Literary Response: Identify events that advance the plot and determine how each event explains or foreshadows actions

What's Your Opinion?

"Argument Sticks" tells the tale of two brothers. With a partner, discuss an argument you have had with a friend or brother or sister. How did you resolve it? Do you think using the argument sticks would have helped you solve your conflict?

Launch into Grammar

Gerunds Words ending in *ing* that are used as nouns are called **gerunds**.

> **Example:** **Arguing** is usually a waste of time.
> (*arguing* is the subject)
> The boys' mother hates **arguing**.
> (*arguing* is the direct object)

All gerunds have an *ing* ending. But not all words with an *ing* ending are gerunds. Words with *ing* endings can also be participles. With a partner, rewrite the sentences below on a separate sheet of paper. Circle all of the gerunds. If an *ing* word is not a gerund, underline it.

1. Fighting never solves problems.

Written conventions: Identify and correctly use various parts of speech

2. The boys' mother loves solving a tough problem.

3. The boys were fighting over some silly thing.

 For more practice using gerunds, use page 75 in the Student Workbook.

Launch into Word Analysis

Antonyms   The opposite of any word is its **antonym**. For example, the word *slow* is the antonym of the word *fast*.

Below are nine words from the story. With a partner, find each word in the story. Then, think of an antonym for each word. Write your words on a separate sheet of paper.

1. wrong	**4.** up	**7.** winner
2. remembered	**5.** first	**8.** north
3. over	**6.** in	**9.** all

 For more practice with antonyms, use page 76 of the Student Workbook.

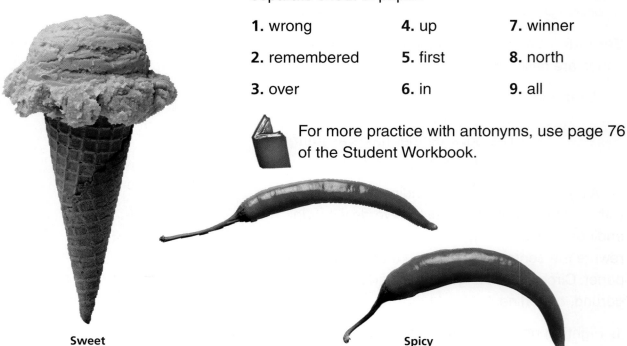

Sweet

Spicy

Reading: Understand and explain common antonyms

Launch into Writing

Identify the main ideas Main ideas are typically placed at the beginning of a paragraph. They should be written in clear, direct language so that the reader makes no mistake about what the point of the paragraph is.

> The mother of the two Iroquois boys used a time-honored trick for of solving an argument—distraction. Why does distraction work? Emotions cause a person to become unreasonable. As powerful as emotions are, they do not last very long. So if you can get people thinking about something else, emotion runs its course, and the problem solves itself.

Make sure that the main ideas in your writing are supported by facts and details. Link the main ideas from several paragraphs together to express the theme of your work.

On a separate sheet of paper, write a short folktale or an essay about the selection you have read. Make sure that each paragraph you write has a clear main idea. When you finish, exchange papers with a partner and identify each other's main ideas.

 For more practice with main ideas, use pages 78–79 of the Student Workbook.

Writing Tip

Poets often use similes and metaphors. With a few words when you write poetry, you can create a picture in your audience's mind. Poets create images that explain without the use of figurative language. You, too, with the use of similes and metaphors, can create one image that can explain much more than an entire sentence can.

Argument Sticks 127

11

**an excerpt from a novel
by Sarah Hayes**

Before You Read

Background

Have you ever wondered who Robin Hood was and how he became the leader of the men of Sherwood Forest? In this excerpt, you will read about the struggles between Prince John and King Richard's men. Also, look out for the older spelling of some words, which the author used to fit the time period.

LEARNING OBJECTIVES

- Recognize foreshadowing
- Recognize analogies
- Learn when you need to capitalize
- Use supporting examples

Building Your Vocabulary

1. With a partner, read over the words that the author used to describe the setting. Use a dictionary for any words you do not know.

    Locksley Farm
    cut-throat
    Sir Guy
    Prince John
    King Richard
    Sheriff of
        Nottingham

Reading: Use a dictionary to find the meaning and other features of unknown words

outlaws   travellers

Sherwood Forest   poachers

2. Using the words in the list, create a chart like the one shown on a separate sheet of paper. Divide the words into two columns. Decide whether they refer to specific people and places or if they are general terms.

People and places	General terms
Sir Guy	*cut-throat*

Reading Strategy

Foreshadowing   Effective stories begin to immediately plant ideas in the reader's mind. This placing of small clues early in a story is called **foreshadowing**. When a writer foreshadows an event, it plants an idea in the reader's mind. For example, a writer could mention dark clouds at the outset of a story. This would set up the reader to expect something later: rain, a storm, or snow.

Applying the Reading Strategy

1. As you read the selection, look for clues for what is to come. Sounds, unusual sights, or puzzling words from a character can all signal more important events later on in the story.

2. When major story events occur, think back to earlier events. Was there anything that might have foreshadowed what was going to happen?

3. Keep in mind that foreshadowing clues can be small or large. Some clues are clear and obvious. Other clues can be minor details that are small and hard to notice.

4. After you finish the story, go back to the beginning and find the clues that foreshadowed what was going to occur.

Robin Hood 129

Robin Hood

an excerpt from a novel by Sarah Hayes

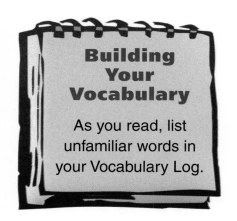

Building Your Vocabulary

As you read, list unfamiliar words in your Vocabulary Log.

Trapped

Robert stopped and whistled quietly to his dog. The dog froze. Not ten paces away a hind and fawn were drinking from the stream. A twig crackled in the undergrowth and the hind lifted her head. For a moment she looked at Robert. He was a tall, slightly built young man, with clear grey eyes and a cheerful grin. As the deer turned to run, Robert heard the unmistakable sound of a bowstring. An arrow whistled out of the trees behind him. The deer staggered and then fell.

Robert was horrified. "Only cowards shoot hinds and fawns!" he shouted. "Come out of the forest and show yourself, coward!" In the next moment he felt his arm pinned behind his back. As he struggled, another man rushed out of the bushes and seized his bow. "Robert Locksley," he said, "you are charged with killing the King's deer. You will be taken before the Sheriff and sentenced to death."

"The hind had a young fawn," said Robert indignantly. "I could never have shot her!"

"But you did," said a cold voice. A man on a black horse rode forward and stood over him. "There are witnesses."

Robert looked up and recognised the thin face and deep-set eyes of Sir Guy of Gisborne. He realised that he had been trapped. Sir Guy and his men must have tracked him into the forest and waited for the right moment.

"The Sheriff takes an interest in poachers," said Sir Guy, "especially those like you who have been heard to speak ill of our noble lord, Prince John."

hind: female of the red deer

Reading: Make and confirm predictions about text by using ideas presented in the text itself, including foreshadowing clues

"That cut-throat," Robert muttered.

"As I expected, a traitor as well as a poacher," Sir Guy said smoothly. "Prince John will be so pleased to hear of your death."

Robert watched the motherless fawn run into the forest. If only he could escape so easily. He knew that Sir Guy and the Sheriff of Notthingham wished him dead. Sir Guy had long wanted to get his hands on Locksley Farm. And the Sheriff had orders to kill anyone who breathed a word against Prince John. It was high time King Richard returned from fighting the Saracens, thought Robert. England had become an evil place in his absence.

Two mail-clad men bound Robert's hands and attached them to a long rope. Sir Guy tied the rope to his saddle and kicked his horse into a fast trot. Half running, half stumbling along at the end of the rope, Robert felt like a dancing bear. He looked up at the canopy of leaves and wondered whether he would ever see the great oaks of Sherwood Forest again.

As the path widened into a clearing, an owl hooted from a tree on the right. Another called from the left. Strange to hear owls in the middle of the day, thought Robert. Then it happened. Two figures leapt down from an enormous oak and pulled Sir Guy off his horse. A little man ran forward and seized Sir Guy's sword. Ten more men surrounded the mail-clad soldiers. Robert had heard people

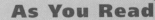

As You Read

1. From reading the story, who do you think the Saracens are? Look them up in the dictionary.

2. How is Robert trapped?

3. What is the penalty for poaching? Does this seem fair?

traitor: one who betrays the trust of a higher authority

It was high time King Richard returned: King Richard should return soon

canopy: the upper layer of a forest

Robin Hood 131

Reading: Make and confirm predictions about text by using ideas presented in the text itself, including foreshadowing clues

speak of forest robbers, but he had never seen them before. They looked a fierce and unkempt bunch.

A tall man came forward. He was dressed in a faded russet uniform. With one slash of his sword, he cut the leather purse from Sir Guy's belt. As he raised his sword again, Robert shouted, "Stop! You have what you want. There is no need to kill him."

The tall man whirled round. "Who are you to give the orders?" he said.

Robert answered him with a question. "Who are you to kill an unarmed man?"

The tall man hesitated. There was something about the young man's open face and serious grey eyes that made him feel ashamed. He sheathed his sword, and left Sir Guy of Gisborne moaning on the ground. Then he murmured something to the little man, who vanished into the forest still waving Sir Guy's sword.

"Jack and Ned, stay behind," the tall man ordered. He unfastened the rope from the black horse's saddle. "As for this bearcub, he shall come with us." He gave a sudden pull on the rope and Robert lost his balance. "Can you do any other tricks, cub?" he asked and laughed. Then, as silently as they had come, all but two of the robbers melted back into the forest. And Robert Locksley went with them.

Half an hour later, however, the little man returned with several coils of rope, and Sir Guy and his soldiers were made ready for their return journey. The forest robbers were well pleased with

unkempt: not neat or tidy
sheathed: put back in a case

Reading: Make and confirm predictions about text by using ideas presented in the text itself, including foreshadowing clues

their handiwork, but Sir Guy did not look happy as he rode into Nottingham. He stared straight ahead and pretended not to notice the gasps of stifled laughter which followed him through the town and up to the gates of the Sheriff's castle.

The Sheriff's Present

In the late afternoon the Sheriff of Nottingham sat alone at his table. It was not a cold day, but the Sheriff was wearing several layers of clothing and a short fur-trimmed cape. He was a little fat man who always felt the cold. Even now a huge fire blazed in the hearth.

The Sheriff was annoyed. Sir Guy was late and he had been forced to eat alone. The stuffed peacocks had been very good, but he had eaten too many of them. The Sheriff picked his teeth and his servants waited for him to shout at them.

Everyone heard the gates clang in the courtyard below. The Sheriff stood up. Gisborne was here at last! And if all had gone well, that fellow Locksley would now be his prisoner. The Sheriff could hear shouting and laughing in the courtyard. He hurried over to the window and looked out. He had to stand on tiptoe to see into the courtyard, and for a moment he did not believe the scene which met his eyes. He blinked and looked again.

Below him stumbled a little procession of exhausted men and horses. Sir Guy and one of his men had been tied back to back and set on Sir Guy's black charger.

The horse hung its head and dragged its feet as if ashamed of its burden. The other soldiers had been

As You Read

1. What do you think it means that the townspeople "stifled laughter" when Sir Guy rode into Nottingham?

2. What do you think Sir Guy's black charger is? Use your dictionary if you need to.

handiwork: work done with personal skill
burden: load

Robin Hood 133

Reading: Make and confirm predictions about text by using ideas presented in the text itself, including foreshadowing clues

roped together in a line to follow along behind, and a little pack-pony completed the cavalcade.

The Sheriff was beside himself with rage. He flew down the stone steps into the courtyard. "What is the meaning of this?" he shrieked. Sir Guy did not reply, but the Sheriff could read his answer on the parchment pinned to the pack-pony's saddle-cloth:

A present to the sheriff
From the men of Sherwood

"What does it mean?" he shouted. "Who are the men of Sherwood? And where is Locksley? What does it mean?" he repeated.

"It means," said Sir Guy slowly, "that Robert Locksley is taken."

"Taken!" shrieked the Sheriff. "Taken where?"

"Taken by forest robbers," replied Sir Guy.

"Is he dead?" asked the Sheriff eagerly. "Are we rid of him at last?"

Sir Guy nodded. He did not know for certain that Locksley was dead, but the tall robber looked a murderous fellow. Young Locksley would be dead before nightfall, he was sure. The Sheriff began to feel more cheerful. He was not fond of Sir Guy, but the man had proved useful to him on more than one occasion. "You are late for dinner, Gisborne," he said testily. But Sir Guy was beyond caring. As a servant loosened his bonds, he slipped down from his horse and fell to the ground in a faint.

parchment: paper made of animal skin
testily: in an annoyed manner

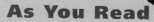

As You Read

1. What is the meaning of the parchment pinned to the pony's saddle-cloth?

2. Does the Sheriff like Sir Guy?

3. Read over the descriptions of the Sheriff. Is he a very likeable character?

4. Who is the leader of the forest robbers?

Reading: Make and confirm predictions about text by using ideas presented in the text itself, including foreshadowing clues

The Greenwood

Twelve miles from Nottingham, in the heart of Sherwood Forest, a young man with keen grey eyes sat beside a roaring fire. Robert Locksley was very much alive. The robbers had untied his hands as soon as they had reached their camp, and given him a fine supper. Now they wanted to know all about the young man who had dared to defy their leader—the tall man they called Will Scarlet.

"There is little to tell," said Robert. "Locksley Farm came to me from my father, and his father before him. Now it is in the hands of Sir Guy of Gisborne; and I am an outlaw, like yourselves."

"We are proud to call ourselves outlaws," Will said quietly, "for much wickedness is done in the name of the law these days."

"Death to Prince John!" shouted a black-bearded man from the circle round the fire.

"Death to the Sheriff!" roared someone else. Then everyone began shouting together until the tall man held up his hand. He turned to Robert. "We are for the King," he said.

"And I," said Robert simply. "May he soon return."

The tall man again held up his hand. "We men of Sherwood have been forced to leave our homes and families, to choose a new way of life here in the forest."

"And kill innocent travellers for gold?" interrupted Robert.

Will tried to explain. "We take only from those who have stolen from others," he said.

As You Read

1. How did Robert get Locksley Farm?

2. Why are the robbers proud to be called "outlaws"?

defy: challenge

outlaws: people who do not follow rules or laws

Robin Hood 135

"And end up thieves and murderers," Robert added.

"They are all brave men," said Will. But the outlaws were silent. The young man made them feel uncomfortable.

Robert broke the silence. "I have seen the faces of the poor," he said. "They are not free like you. They are tied forever to cruel masters like Sir Guy of Gisborne. The little they have is taken from them by the men of power."

"By the Sheriff, more like," someone said.

"Aye, and that fat Abbot at St. Mary's," added the little man.

"Quiet, Much," said Will. He was listening intently.

"Steal from the rich, by all means," continued Robert, "they have more than enough. But why not give back to the poor what has been taken from them?"

"Rob the rich to feed the poor," said the black-bearded man, "is that what you mean?"

"I think so," said Robert in some confusion. He had not meant to give a speech.

"Will you join us here in the forest?" asked Will suddenly.

Robert laughed. "I think I have no choice," he answered. "But I have much to learn."

"First you should have a new name," said Will. Then he smiled. "You must forgive the rough treatment in the forest: with any luck the Sheriff thinks you dead by now. He must not hear the name of Locksley again." He looked

Abbot: the head of a monastery, a place where monks live

Reading: Make and confirm predictions about text by using ideas presented in the text itself, including foreshadowing clues

down at his suit of faded russet, and added, "I was not born to the name of Will Scarlet."

"Nor I Jack Smithy," said the man with the beard.

"They call me Much the Miller," said the little man.

Will looked at Robert. "What do you say to Robin O'Greenwood?" he asked.

"Too long," muttered Jack Smithy.

"Robin Wood?" suggested Robert.

"We have a Wood already," a new voice said. "Thomas Wood of Dale."

Robert pulled his cloak over his head and grinned. "Shall it be Robin Hood, then?"

"Aye," said Will, "Robin Hood will do."

"Robin Hood is good," said Jack Smithy, who was somewhat too fond of the sound of his own voice. "But what can Robin Hood give us in return for his new name? He looks hardly more than a boy."

"I can plough a straight furrow," said Robin.

"In the forest!" said Jack in disgust.

"I can tell a good cow."

"Deer are the only beasts in Sherwood," Jack growled.

"I can use a bow," said Robin. "My father taught me."

"Not so well as Will, I'll bet," said someone.

The tall man stepped into the firelight. "I am glad to meet a fellow archer," he said. "Tomorrow we shall test your skill."

The robbers were impatient. "The wand, the wand," they shouted. "Let us have the contest now." Robin's father had told him about the wand. It was a whippy length of peeled willow

plough: to turn over and break up dirt

furrow: a trench in the earth

Robin Hood 137

nailed to a tree, almost impossible to hit in broad daylight. Now night was falling fast.

"Jack found your bow in the forest," said Will, and the black-bearded man handed Robin his beloved silver-tipped bow. Robin peered into the gloom. The wand was barely visible. He took aim and shot. His arrow landed a finger's breadth from the wand. Will's arrow landed quivering between Robin's and the wand. The robbers roared their approval. Robin took a deep breath and shot again. This time the arrow flew straight to the wand and split it clean in two. The robbers gasped.

"Not bad for a farmer's boy," said Jack.

Will bowed. "I have never split the wand," he said.

"Nor had I before this moment," said Robin. He had surprised himself.

In the months that followed, the outlaws taught Robin everything they knew. He learned how to walk silently in the forest paths, how to hoot like an owl and how to wait for hours in the rain wedged in the fork of a tree. He learned how to fight with knives, how to wrestle, and how to tell a good story.

Robin felt that he had little to offer in return: a keen eye and a sure aim, that was all. But he was wrong. The outlaws found in Robin something that had been missing from their lives. The young man's enthusiasm, his sense of fun and his gentle ways reminded them of the homes

As You Read

1. What are some things Robin learns from the outlaws?

2. Why does Robin become the "undisputed" leader? What do you think "undisputed" means?

breadth: width

fork: place where a branch meets a tree trunk

Reading: Make and confirm predictions about text by using ideas presented in the text itself, including foreshadowing clues

and families they had lost. Soon Robin became the undisputed leader of the band.

Within a year over a hundred men had come to Sherwood. They were no longer a dirty, dishevelled band of robbers but a highly trained army, dressed in Lincoln green and dedicated to Robin's rallying call—rob the rich to feed the poor. Many a starving peasant had his grain sack mysteriously filled, and hungry families found food waiting on their doorsteps. People began to talk with awe about Robin Hood and the men of Sherwood. But while the poor folk rejoiced, the rich grew angry. Two men in particular feared and hated the name of Robin Hood—a cold-voiced knight and a little fat man with a gold chain—Sir Guy of Gisborne and the Sheriff of Nottingham.

Connecting to History

King Richard I (also called Richard the Lionhearted) was born on Sept. 8, 1157. He was raised in Aquitaine, a part of southern France, so English was not his first language. Richard became King in 1189, when his brother Henry died, but he didn't spend very much time at home. Between 1189 and 1199 he spent only six months in England. He left his brother, Earl John, in charge of his estates while he went off to fight in the Crusades.

dishevelled: disorderly
rallying: renewing or motivating

About the Author

Sarah Hayes
Sarah Hayes is the author of many books for children and young adults, including *Nine Ducks Nine* and *The Cats of Tiffany Street*.

Reading: Make and confirm predictions about text by using ideas presented in the text itself, including foreshadowing clues

After You Read

Retell It!

Do you think the Sheriff of Nottingham and Sir Guy of Gisborne feel that they are villains, or the "bad guys," in the reading? With a partner, rewrite the story from the point of view of the Sheriff and Sir Guy.

Think, Discuss, Write

Discuss the following questions in small groups. Write your answers on a separate sheet of paper.

1. **Setting**   When do you think this story takes place? What clues in the reading let you know?

2. **Make inferences**   Why do you think Robert stops the robber from killing Gisborne?

3. **Word analysis**   What does the phrase "melted back into the forest" on page 132 mean?

4. **Recall details**   Who does the Sheriff see tied up as he looks out his window into the courtyard?

5. **Recall details**   Describe what the robbers do to Sir Guy and his men.

6. **Compare and contrast**   How is the writing in this reading different from a story that is set in modern times?

7. **Connect themes**   This unit is called "Conflict." Could the excerpt you just read have been used in the "Friendship" and "Courage" units of this book? Why or why not?

Test-Taking Tip

Here are some tips that will help you succeed when you are taking a multiple-choice test.

- Read the question or statement carefully. Then think of the answer before you look at your choices.

- Read all of the choices before you pick one.

- If you do not see an answer that you like, cross out the answers that you know are wrong.

- Do not spend too much time on a question that you cannot answer.

Reading: Ask questions and support answers by connecting prior knowledge with information from the text

What's Your Opinion?

Answer the questions below on a separate sheet of paper. Use your answers to write a review of the excerpt. Make a presentation to the class in which you discuss your reaction to the story.

1. The story was _____ interesting.
   a. extremely   **c.** a little
   b. very   **d.** not at all

2. The language in the story was _____.
   a. challenging but not too hard
   b. a little bit difficult   **c.** very difficult

3. I was able to understand the story _____.
   a. completely   **c.** a little bit
   b. more or less   **d.** not at all

Launch into Grammar

Capitalization   Capital letters should be used: (a) at the beginning of a sentence, (b) for proper nouns and the pronoun *I*, (c) for names and titles, and (d) for abbreviations.

   With a partner, find the words that should be capitalized. Rewrite the sentences on a separate sheet of paper.

1. an arrow whistled out of the trees behind him.

2. he knew that sir guy and the sheriff of nottingham wished him dead.

Written conventions: Capitalize the first word of a sentence, names of people, and the pronoun *I*

3. it was high time king richard returned from fighting the saracens, thought robert.

4. in the heart of sherwood forest, a young man with keen grey eyes sat before a fire.

 For more practice with capitalization, use page 83 in the Student Workbook.

Launch into Word Analysis

Analogies An analogy is a special relationship between two pairs of items. The items themselves may be different, but the link, or relationship, between the items is the same. For example:

Forest is to **tree** as **army** is to **soldier**.

In the analogy above, a forest is made of trees in the same way that an army is made of soldiers. With a partner, write a word to complete each analogy on a separate sheet of paper.

1. **King** is to **England** as **president** is to _____.

2. **Bow** is to **arrow** as **paintbrush** is to _____.

3. **Owl** is to **night** as **rooster** is to _____.

4. **Sheriff** is to **outlaw** as **cat** is to _____.

Work with a partner to complete these analogies. Write your analogies on your paper.

dog : puppy : :   sun : hot : :
ice : water : :   sink : kitchen : :

 For more practice with analogies, use page 84 of the Student Workbook.

Reading: Classify grade-appropriate categories of words

Launch into Writing

Use supporting examples   One way to make your writing more interesting is to use **examples**. Examples help you make your descriptions and explanations crystal clear. Take a look at the following paragraph.

> Sir Guy of Gisborne was not an honorable man. To see just how treacherous he was, remember how he captured Robert. First, Sir Guy had his men kill the mother of a baby deer. Then, Sir Guy blamed the killing on Robin. First, he did something wrong. Then, he lied about it. And in his lie, he blamed the misdeed on someone else!

Rather than just describe Sir Guy using negative terms, this paragraph uses an example to *show* his treacherous deeds. With a partner, write a paragraph on a separate sheet of paper that involves Robin Hood. In your paragraph, use two or more examples.

 For more practice with supporting examples, use pages 86–87 of the Student Workbook.

Writing: Write responses to literature: Demonstrate an understanding of the work, and support judgments through references

12

Before You Read

Zlata's Diary

**diary entries by
Zlata Filipović**

Background

Zlata was eleven years old when she began writing her diary in September 1991. This was right before war broke out in Sarajevo, the capital of Bosnia and Herzegovina (usually referred to as Bosnia). She continued to write in her diary until October 1993. She wrote as if she were writing letters to a friend named Mimmy. In this excerpt from her diary, you will learn about how the war changed her life and affected her family. Do you have a diary? Does it help you to work out conflicts?

LEARNING OBJECTIVES

- Distinguish between fact and opinion
- Recognize hyphens and dashes
- Recognize symbols
- Quote other sources

Building Your Vocabulary

Listed below are some idioms that you will find in "Zlata's Diary." Discuss these idioms with your partner. Have you ever heard them used? Write down their meanings. If you are not sure, guess. Then go back and check what you wrote once you have read the selection.

Example: for ages   **Answer:**   a long time

walking my feet off   war is still on
I'll give it my all   why on Earth
brings me back to earth   playing games

Reading: Identify and interpret figurative language and words with multiple meanings

Sarajevo.

Reading Strategy

Distinguish fact and opinion   A *fact* is a statement that can be proven to be true. An *opinion* describes a feeling, belief, or judgment. For example, it is a fact that Sarajevo hosted the Winter Olympics in 1984. It is an opinion that the war in Sarajevo could have been avoided. When you read, make sure that you can tell the difference between facts and opinions.

Applying the Reading Strategy

1. Keep on the lookout for facts and opinions as you begin to read. Facts are statements that are (or could be) backed up. Look for names, dates, and past events to be facts.

2. Look for clue words to introduce opinions: *I think, I believe, In my opinion,* and so on. Strong description words also often state opinions: *I really like, It is beautiful, best, worst, good,* and *bad.*

3. In most cases, accept facts to be true. With opinions, be more cautious. Make your own judgment on an opinion after you weigh the evidence.

4. Keep looking for facts, examples, and other forms of evidence to both support and challenge the facts and opinions you come across.

Zlata's Diary

diary entries by Zlata Filipović

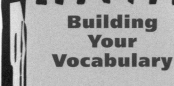

Building Your Vocabulary

As you read, list unfamiliar words in your Vocabulary Log.

As You Read

1. How many months have passed since the last time Zlata saw her piano teacher?

2. Who are Czerny, Bach, Mozart, and Chopin?

3. What is "not going to be easy"?

Monday, December 28, 1992
Dear Mimmy,
   I've been walking my feet off these past few days.
   I'm at home today. I had my first piano lesson. My teacher and I kissed and hugged, we hadn't seen each other since March. Then we moved on to Czerny, Bach, Mozart and Chopin to the étude, the invention, the sonata and the "piece." It's not going to be easy. But I'm not going to school now and I'll give it my all. It makes me happy. Mimmy, I'm now in my fifth year of music school.
   You know, Mimmy, we've had no water or electricity for ages. When I go out and when there's no shooting it's as if the war were over, but this business with the electricity and water, this darkness, this winter, the shortage of wood and food, brings me back to earth and then I realize that the war is still on. Why? Why on earth don't those "kids" come to some agreement? They really are playing games. And it's us they're playing with.
   As I sit writing to you, my dear Mimmy, I look over at Mommy and Daddy. They are reading. They lift their eyes from the page and think about something. What are they thinking about? About the book they are reading or are they trying to put

étude: a piece of music for the practice of technique
invention: a short composition with two or three part counterpoint
sonata: a composition of three or four movements in contrasting forms and keys

Reading: Distinguish facts and opinions in text

together the scattered pieces of this war puzzle? I think it must be the latter. Somehow they look even sadder to me in the light of the oil lamp (we have no more wax candles, so we make our own oil lamps). I look at Daddy. He really has lost a lot of weight. The scales say twenty-five kilos [fifty-five pounds], but looking at him I think it must be more. I think even his glasses are too big for him. Mommy has lost weight too. She's shrunk somehow, the war has given her wrinkles. God, what is this war doing to my parents? They don't look like my old Mommy and Daddy anymore. Will this ever stop? Will our suffering stop so that my parents can be what they used to be—cheerful, smiling, nice-looking?

This stupid war is destroying my childhood, it's destroying my parents' lives. Why? Stop the war! I need peace!

I'm going to play a game of cards with them!

Love from your Zlata.

latter: the second or last thing referred to

About the Author
Zlata Filipović (b. 1980)

Zlata Filipović began keeping her diary at the age of eleven, in September of 1991, shortly before the shelling of Sarajevo began. In her diary, she recorded her experiences and observations in war-torn Bosnia. Zlata continued to write in her diary until 1993, when her family moved to France.

Reading: Distinguish facts and opinions in text

After You Read

Retell It!

With a partner, suppose that one of you is Zlata and the other is a close friend. Have a phone conversation about conditions in Sarajevo. The friend should ask questions that will allow Zlata to give the important details from her diary entry.

Think, Discuss, Write

Discuss the following questions in small groups. Write your answers on a separate sheet of paper.

1. **Structure**   This reading is written in the form of a diary entry. How is this similar to a letter?

2. **Recall details**   How many years has Zlata been taking music lessons? Why do you think they make her happy?

3. **Recall details**   Describe what Zlata's parents look like.

4. **Compare and contrast**   How has the war changed Zlata's parents?

5. **Make inferences**   Write down all the questions that Zlata asks Mimmy. Do you think Zlata really knows the answers to those questions?

6. **Tone**   The tone of Zlata's writing could be considered conversational. What makes this writing different from the writing of a story?

7. **Predict**   How do you think Zlata's childhood experience will affect her adult life?

Reading: Recognize cause-and-effect relationships in a text

What's Your Opinion?

Did you like reading this diary entry? On a separate sheet of paper, draw a chart like the one here to show what you liked and what you did not like about the selection. Compare your chart with your classmates' charts.

Liked	Didn't Like

Launch into Grammar

Hyphens and dashes   Hyphens and dashes look similar, but they have different functions in a sentence. Hyphens are used to break up words at the end of a line. Most words should be divided into syllables between the two consonants, if possible, or between a root word and a suffix.

> walk- ing   some- how   sad- der   cheer- ful

Hyphens are also used to connect words to make compound adjectives.

> nice-looking   fun-loving

Dashes are longer than hyphens. They are used to show a sharp change in thought in a sentence. They are also used to set off information in a sentence.

> Why can't my parents be what they used to be—cheerful and smiling?

Written conventions: Use knowledge of the basic rules of punctuation when writing

Our leader—a man we don't trust—came on TV to speak.

With a partner, find where hyphens and dashes are used in the reading. Write the examples on a separate sheet of paper. Then make up one more example using hyphens and dashes.

 For more practice with hyphens and dashes, use page 91 of the Student Workbook.

Launch into Word Analysis

Symbols   In literature, a single word, image, or thing can represent, or be the **symbol** of, something else. A dove is often recognized to be the symbol of peace. The sun can stand for hope.

In "Zlata's Diary," several items can be considered as symbols. With a partner, identify the symbols brought up in the questions below. Write your responses on a separate sheet of paper.

1. The beauty of music cannot be harmed by events in the outside world. What does *music* symbolize?

2. The city is dark because there is no electricity. What might *darkness* symbolize?

3. Daddy is losing so much weight he seems to be shrinking away. What might *Daddy's weight loss* symbolize?

 Work in a group. Reread *Zlata's Diary*. Talk about the ways that Zlata describes wars and the people who wage them.

Reading: Understand and explain the figurative and metaphorical use of words in context

For more practice with symbols, use page 92 in the Student Workbook.

Launch into Writing

Quote other sources When you write nonfiction, you often need to back up important facts and opinions by quoting other sources. The sources you quote could include books, newspapers, magazine articles, web sites, and experts on the subject you are writing about. When you actually record the words of a source, put the words in quotation marks. Otherwise, simply make sure that you identify the source you are using. Example:

> The publication Audiofile describes Zlata's Diary as a work in which eleven-year old Zlata "describes her life in Sarajevo as the clouds of war build, advance and consume her city."

Write your own review of *Zlata's Diary.* Use quotations from sources that you find on the Internet, or in a newspaper or magazine. With a partner, write your review on a separate sheet of paper.

 For more practice with quoting sources, use pages 94–95 of the Student Workbook.

Writing: Quote or paraphrase information sources, citing them appropriately

Deliver an Oral Summary

Work in a small group and take turns summarizing one of the readings from this unit. Remember that a summary is a brief statement of the main ideas written in your own words.

Read over the four readings: "Class Bully," "Argument Sticks," "Robin Hood," and "Zlata's Diary."

Step One: Plan Your Summary

1. Decide which reading you will summarize.

2. Reread the selection. Review your class notes. What is the basic plot or topic of the reading?

3. Identify the main idea of the reading you selected. Note important details to support the main idea. Include the names of the characters, the basic plot, the setting, and the main idea. Tell how the selection begins, how the main idea is developed, and how the reading ends. For "Class Bully," focus on the overall meaning of the poem.

4. Use your notes to write your summary. Since your summary will be presented orally in class, you do not need to write out every word. Use notecards to help you recall important information. Include all of the following details.

   - an introduction to the reading including the title, the author's name, and a brief statement about the genre (e.g., fiction, nonfiction, poetry)
   - setting
   - characters
   - conflict
   - resolution

Step Two: Practice Your Summary

Work with a partner. Practice presenting your summary aloud. When you present, your partner should take notes about how you can improve your summary. Partners should also note the best features of the presentation.

Speaking: Deliver oral summaries of books: Include the main ideas and convey a comprehensive understanding of sources

Step Three:
Present Your Summary

Present your summary to the class.
Have one member of your group be
ready to answer questions.

Step Four:
Evaluate Your Summary

Have your audience use the Speaking
Checklist to evaluate the presentation of
your summary.

Record Your Summary

Record your summary. Listen to your
own tape and to the tapes of your
classmates.

Speaking Checklist

✔ I used an appropriate tone of voice.

✔ I spoke slowly enough to be clear,
but not so slowly that I lost my
audience's attention.

✔ I used appropriate posture and
gestures. I did not do anything that
would distract my audience.

✔ I made eye contact with the
audience. I looked at each person
while speaking.

Speaking: Deliver oral summaries of books: Include the main ideas and convey a comprehensive understanding of
sources

Write a Response to Literature

In this unit, you have been reading about different types of conflicts. Did you like what you read? Respond to one of the selections from this unit by writing a review. Include a strong thesis statement that includes your feelings about the selection, support for your feelings, and a clear conclusion. Read the review of *Robin Hood* on this page to help you with your own review.

1. Pre-write

Before you begin writing your review, think about your purpose and audience. What selection will you write about? Who will your readers be? What examples should you use to support your point? Make a cluster map to organize your ideas.

2. Draft

Follow these steps to organize your review.

A. Begin with a strong opening paragraph that states your viewpoint. Use concrete language and a clear organizational pattern.

Review of Robin Hood

Do you know the story of Robin Hood? Have you seen the Disney version on television? Well, Sarah Hayes' Robin Hood is a complete surprise.

Robin Hood is the story of Robert Locksley, a young man who finds himself manipulated by the villain Sir Guy of Gisborne. While Sarah Hayes' story was truly informative and enjoyable, I found some of the text difficult to understand. I had trouble imagining the setting and characters; I felt almost as if some parts of the story were set in modern times. Nevertheless, if you like action adventures, you might like to read Robin Hood.

Writing: Write responses to literature: Demonstrate an understanding of a literary work, and support judgments

B. Give examples to support your viewpoint in your opening paragraph. Organize your ideas in paragraphs.

C. Finish with a concluding paragraph. Restate your viewpoint.

Refer to your cluster map to guide you as you draft your response to literature.

3. Revise

Reread your draft and ask yourself these questions:

- Have I captured my reader's interest in the opening paragraph?
- Have I made my viewpoint clear?
- Have I used specific examples from the selection to support my viewpoint?
- Have I ended with a final paragraph that restates my viewpoint?

4. Edit and Proofread

Proofread your revised essay. Check punctuation, capitalization, and spelling. Look in a dictionary to verify the spelling of any words.

5. Publish

Now you are ready to publish your review. Since reviews are commonly found in newspapers and magazines, consider submitting your review to the school newspaper for publication. Prepare your review in the following way:

A. Make a clean copy of your review using the computer.

B. Make sure that your review has a title, and run the spell check to verify that all words in your review are spelled correctly.

C. Read your review one more time to be sure it states what you intended.

Writing: Revise writing to improve the organization and consistency of ideas within and between paragraphs

News Story

Project Goal

In this unit you read about conflict and how people come together to **resolve** conflicts. For this project, you will research a current or past **conflict** in the news and present a short news story about it.

1. Look in a newspaper or on the Internet for news **coverage** on any type of conflicts in the news. Look for information on wars between countries, such as in the Middle East, and **disputes** and conflict in cities, counties, and neighborhoods. Look for stories about politicians or people who are arguing over laws, the rights of others, housing problems, lawsuits, education problems, and so on.

   With a partner, make a list and answer the following questions:

   • Who is involved in the conflict?

   • Why are they arguing or in conflict?

   • Are they trying to peacefully resolve their problems by discussing them or trying to compromise? How are they attempting to resolve their problems?

2. Write a short news story. Include a few paragraphs explaining what the conflict is. Tell who is involved, what it is about, and where it is happening. Read the news stories you find in the paper or on the Internet to see how they are written. Make sure that you include a main sentence, an interesting introduction, sentences providing examples and evidence of your main sentence. Finish with a clear conclusion that sums up what is going on now with this problem and how it is or is not being resolved.

3. Include pictures in your story. Cut them out of the newspaper or download them from the Internet.

4. Present your story to the class.

Words to Know

resolve
conflict
disputes
coverage

Writing: Write expository descriptions of a real person, place, or event, using sensory details

Read More About Conflict

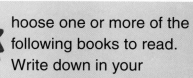

hoose one or more of the following books to read. Write down in your Reading Log the books you read and your opinion of each. Ask yourself the following questions:

1. What type of confict are the characters experiencing?
2. Who is involved?
3. How do they resolve conflict?

Nonfiction

Crews: Gang Members Talk to Maria Hinojosa by Maria Hinojosa

These interviews with young men and women who live in violent and poor U.S. neighborhoods reveal how they deal with the everyday conflicts that surround them.

Why Do They Hate Me?: Young Lives Caught in War and Conflict by Laurel Holliday

The children, who live in war-torn areas, speak in secret diaries, letters, essays, and memoirs. These children's experiences open connections for group discussion about tolerance in the neighborhood and on the international front.

Fiction

My Man Blue by Nikki Grimes

In fourteen poems, read about an African-American boy living in a difficult neighborhood, and the man who helps keep his feet grounded and his self-esteem steady against the occasional buffeting of his peers.

To Kill a Mockingbird by Harper Lee

This classic novel features Scout, a young girl, who tells the story of life in a small southern town. Read about her father's decision to defend an African-American man who he believes innocent of the crime of which he is accused, although much of the town thinks he is guilty.

Reading: Compare and contrast information on the same topic

UNIT 4
Goals

"In America, anybody can become somebody."

—Jesse Owens
(American athlete, 1913–1980)

Discuss the Theme
Achieving Goals

Some goals take a lifetime to achieve, but there are also goals
that can be achieved in just one day. When we set goals for
ourselves, we have a purpose for our work. In this unit, you will
learn how to set up an E-mail address. You will also read about
a girl who has set herself the goal of winning a scholarship
jacket. In "Racing a Champion," you will learn how one person
achieved the goal of becoming a great swimmer. Finally, you
will read a poem entitled "Marathon" about a person who finds
inspiration in the achievements of others. As you read this unit,
think about these questions:

- What is it that you do well?
- What are your goals and dreams for the future?
- What can you do to achieve those goals?
- What does success mean to you?

WRITING FOCUS:
Write a Research Report

13

Setting Up an E-Mail Address

an excerpt from a nonfiction book by Larry P. Stevens and Cara J. Stevens

Before You Read

Background

Do you have an E-mail address? If not, have you ever sent or received an E-mail message? Is one of your goals to have a computer some day or to use an E-mail address? Would you like to E-mail friends, relatives, or people in other countries? In this reading, you will learn *what you can get* from an E-mail address, *the cost*, and *the terms* used for the Internet and E-mail addresses.

LEARNING OBJECTIVES

- Understand simple technical directions
- Use parentheses and brackets
- Recognize compound words
- Recognize topic sentences

Building Your Vocabulary

1. This reading uses many terms related to setting up and having an E-mail account. With a partner, read the following words from the article. Discuss the meanings of the words you know. Use a dictionary to check the meanings of words you do not know.

modem	service	domain
network	access	extension
ports	sites	

Writing: Demonstrate familiarity with computer terminology

2. Some of the words have more than one meaning. On a separate sheet of paper, create a chart like the one below. Using the reading and a dictionary, write down two meanings for each word.

	Common Meaning	Technical Computer-related Meaning
modem	a device that converts signals	a device that converts signals between computer and phone
domain	complete ownership of land	name and location of E-mail service provider

Reading Strategy

Understand technical directions   You need to follow directions to do such things as: setting your watch to the right time, putting a table together, using a power tool, or playing a video game. To make sure that you follow directions correctly, take a look at the steps below.

Applying the Reading Strategy

1. Start by scanning the directions from beginning to end. What is the goal of the directions? How long will it take to reach this goal? Do you have everything you need to start and finish the job?

2. Follow each step carefully. Finish each step completely before you go on to the next step.

3. If you make a mistake, don't panic. Work backwards to find out what went wrong.

4. When you finish the job, look back over the directions. Did you miss anything? Did you accomplish the goal? Does the item work the way it is supposed to work?

Reading: Follow multiple-step instructions in a basic technical manual

Setting Up an E-Mail Address

an excerpt from a nonfiction book by
Larry P. Stevens and Cara J. Stevens

An E-mail address is basically your own personal mailbox. It is the face that you present to the Internet community. It can reflect your personality, your interests, and even your dreams. Read on to discover how to make your address your own.

What Do I Need to Get E-mail?

1. Access to a Macintosh® or IBM®-compatible computer, or cable-based E-mail
2. A modem, which is usually used at home, or access to a network, which is found either in company offices or at schools
3. An Internet Service Provider (ISP) or network connection
4. An account with an E-mail provider

Do I Need to Have My Own Personal Computer?

As much as we'd like to help you out and ask your parents to buy you a computer immediately so you can get E-mail—which you absolutely can't live without—we can't do that because we would be lying. (Sorry!)

The good news is that all you need is access to a computer that's able to connect to the Internet, whether it belongs to your family, a friend, or a library, school, or other public place. And if your family uses a cable-based Internet service such as WebTV®, you don't even need a computer. WebTV® allows you to hook up E-mail and Internet access to any basic television set, as long as it has the proper connection ports. This is a fantastic way to obtain E-mail access if you don't want to purchase a computer.

Building Your Vocabulary

As you read, list unfamiliar words in your Vocabulary Log.

As You Read

1. What does ISP stand for?
2. What are the advantages of using WebTV®?

Reading: Follow multiple-step instructions in a basic technical manual

The Costs of E-mail

An E-mail service can cost money, but it doesn't have to. Thanks to how popular E-mail has become and how easy it is for companies to provide, some companies offer free services in exchange for information or a purchase of something else.

Ways to Cut Down the Costs

- **Free Computers:** Some companies offer you a free computer if you pay for a certain number of years of Internet service in advance.

- **Special Offers:** Offers pop up all the time, so alert your parents to be on the lookout for special opportunities.

- **Free Internet Service Only** (you must have a computer): Some services offer free Internet access. The catch is that they sell advertisements that flash in a window on your screen whenever you log on. Advertisers pay the cost of your Internet access.

- **Free E-mail:** There are a lot of Web sites that offer free E-mail. In fact, many of your favorite sites may offer free E-mail accounts. These sites gather up information and offer an easier way for Internet users to find their way through the Web. Go to your favorite sites and see if they offer free E-mail addresses. The best providers to go with are the well-known ones that have been around a while. Smaller sites may not be around very long, and may go out of business or change their name without warning.

catch: a hidden disadvantage

Reading: Follow multiple-step instructions in a basic technical manual

The Parts of an E-mail Address

While an E-mail address may be complicated to remember or understand at first, it's actually very simple when you break it down. There are three elements to an E-mail address, and all three are equally important. The first is the *username;* the second (after the @ symbol) is the *domain name;* and the third (after the dot) is the *extension.*

$$\underset{1}{\text{Username}}@\underset{2}{\text{Domain}}.\underset{3}{\text{extension}}$$

The address reads from the most specific part (the username) to the most general (the extension).

Username

This is the name that identifies the user, or owner, of the E-mail. Usually the user is allowed to pick a name.

Some people like to just use their first names or initials. Others create addresses based on what they like to do, such as SkiDude@xxx.com or SoccerFan@xx.com. Whatever you choose, pick it to reflect who you are—and be creative. You can showcase your love of a sport, your favorite sports team, your favorite hobby, or your favorite character from a book. There are a few rules that will help you pick a name that's easy to remember, and safe as well.

Choose a name that
- is easy to spell without looking it up;
- doesn't have numbers or strange made-up words in it (flurgleoog863 probably wouldn't be the best choice);
- is easy to remember; and
- doesn't have information that can tell someone where they can find you, such as your last name, town, school, or Little League team.

showcase: emphasize

Reading: Follow multiple-step instructions in a basic technical manual

Domain Name

The part of the E-mail address after the @ symbol is called the domain name. It tells you who is providing the E-mail service and where the mail servers (the E-mail post office boxes we mentioned earlier) are located. The domain name tells the Internet where to look for the computer that hosts the mail. It works the same way a zip code works when you send a letter. The domain name can be named after

• the Internet Service Provider (ISP)
• the free Internet E-mail provider

There are many different domains you can end up with, depending on the type of E-mail service you select.

Extension

The last part of the address is the extension. It's a three-letter code that tells you something about the type of E-mail service the user has. The most common extensions used in the United States are as follows:

.com, which is used by companies and businesses

.edu, which is used by educational institutions

.gov, which is used by government offices such as the U.S. Food and Drug Administration (fda.gov) and offices of elected officials such as the president, congressmen, and senators

.mil, which is used by the military

.net, which stands for network, and usually signifies an Internet Service Provider

signifies: refers to

As You Read

1. What does the domain name do?

2. Why is it important to have a simple username?

3. What do you think *hosts* means in "for the computer that hosts the mail"?

Reading: Follow multiple-step instructions in a basic technical manual

.org, which is most often used by nonprofit organizations or charities

Some addresses use an international code, such as JP for Japan, US for the United States, AU for Australia, or CA for Canada.

When you send an E-mail to someone, you must include all parts of the address and spell them correctly in order for the E-mail to reach that person. The problem with computers is that they can't recognize simple mistakes the way humans can. If you mix up two letters or use the % symbol instead of the @ symbol, for instance, the E-mail won't get where it is supposed to go.

Protect Your E-mail

When you get an E-mail address, you will be asked to come up with a password. This password will protect your privacy as long as you keep it a secret. When you choose your password, though, make sure you don't keep your password a secret from the most important person— YOU! Write your password where no one can figure out what it's for, perhaps on a piece of paper under your alarm clock or inside your piggy bank, or on a page in your diary.

E-mail Privacy

Think of your E-mail as a postcard or a note you pass to a friend in school, where anything you write can be read by someone else. There are many ways people can read what you have written.

1. E-mail you send is saved in your "Outgoing" or "Sent" box when you have a non-Web-based E-mail account. E-mail you receive is saved in

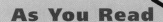

As You Read

1. Why is it important to protect your E-mail?
2. Why is E-mail like a postcard?

piggy bank: a jar used to save coins and dollar bills

Reading: Follow multiple-step instructions in a basic technical manual

your folders. These E-mails can be read by anyone who has access to your computer, even if that person doesn't sign on or have your password.

2. When you e-mail a friend, that E-mail is saved in his or her inbox or folder. Anyone who has access to your friend's computer can read your E-mails.

3. Some free Web-based E-mail programs are targets of hackers, or mischievous people who break into computer systems. Once they break in, they can read any E-mail on the system.

4. Your friend could forward your E-mail to other friends who could send it to their friends who could send it to their friends, and so on.

So don't put anything in an E-mail that you wouldn't want anyone else to read!

About the Authors

Larry P. Stevens and Cara J. Stevens

Larry and Cara Stevens are a writing team. They enjoy writing books that help young people learn how to communicate and accomplish tasks. This excerpt is taken from their book, *The Kids' Guide to E-Mail*.

After You Read

Retell It!

With a partner, go over the steps involved in setting up an E-mail address. Note any directions that seem confusing or unclear to you.

Think, Discuss, Write

Work in small groups. Discuss the questions and write your answers on a separate sheet of paper.

1. **Recall details** What are the three parts of an E-mail address?

2. **Word analysis** Define **E-mail address.** Why do you think E-mail is an important form of communication?

3. **Recall details** Explain what **WebTV®** is. How could you use WebTV®?

4. **Structure** What type of reading have you just read? How does it differ from a story or poem?

5. **Compare and contrast** Compare *username* with *extension.* Which of the two can you usually personalize?

6. **Cause and effect** What could happen if you did not protect your E-mail?

7. **Make inferences** Who pays the cost of free Internet service? Why do you think some people choose not to use the free service?

Reading: Restate facts and details in the text to clarify and organize ideas

Liked	Did Not Like	Reasons For	Reasons Against
I liked learning about free E-mail.	I did not like learning that hackers could read my E-mail.	I learned a lot.	I like reading stories better.

What's Your Opinion?

Work in a small group. Discuss why you did or did not like the reading. Make a chart like the one above on a separate sheet of paper. Your chart should show how the members of your group felt about "Setting Up an E-Mail Address". A reason *for* might be "I learned a lot." A reason *against* might be "I like reading stories better."

Launch into Grammar

Parentheses and brackets   Parentheses and brackets are used to include important, extra information. Commas and other punctuation marks should go outside of the parentheses, except when the information stands as a complete sentence.

Examples: You need an Internet Service Provider (ISP) or network connection.
You can cut costs by having free Internet service only (you must have a computer).

Brackets are used when you want to show one parenthetical phrase inside of another. Brackets are also used to add your own comments to a quote.

Written conventions: Use parentheses

Examples: It's easy to keep track of E-mail addresses (most E-mail services [though not all] have a "Remember This Address" function) on your computer.

Gates said, "We [his company] will see what happens."

With a partner, write down five examples of parentheses from the reading on a separate sheet of paper.

 For more practice using parentheses and brackets, complete page 99 of the Student Workbook.

Launch into Word Analysis

Compound words Compound words are formed by combining two or more words together. Some compound words, like *desktop*, join two words to form a single compound word. Other compound words, like *cable-based*, or *hard drive*, separate the two words with a hyphen or a space.

With a partner, find at least four examples of compound words in the selection. Write them on a sheet of paper in a table like the one below.

Compound word	First Word	Second Word	Meaning
mailbox	mail	box	container for mail

Reading: Use knowledge of individual words in unknown compound words to predict their meaning

For more practice with compound words, complete page 100 of the Student Workbook.

Launch into Writing

Write a topic sentence   In your writing, it is a good idea to begin important paragraphs with a **topic sentence**. The topic sentence tells what the subject, or main idea of the paragraph, will be. Supporting sentences follow the topic sentence. Finally, the paragraph should end with a sentence that brings the topic to a close.

An E-mail address is basically your own personal mailbox.
An E-mail service can cost money, but it doesn't have to.

Write a short article about your experience with E-mail. Do you have your own E-mail account or have you ever used one? Do you know someone who has or uses E-mail? As far as you know, what are the best and worst parts of E-mail? Write your article on a separate sheet of paper. Make sure that each paragraph of your article has a topic sentence.

 For more practice with topic sentences, complete pages 102–103 of the Student Workbook.

Writing: Create a single paragraph: Develop a topic sentence, and include simple supporting facts and details

14

Before You Read

Background

Have you ever set a goal and worked hard to achieve it? How would you feel if an honor or award that you knew you had earned was going to be given to someone else?

In this autobiographical story, you will find out what an eighth grader does when she learns that someone else is to be awarded the scholarship jacket that she has worked hard to win.

The *Scholarship Jacket*

**a story by
Marta Salinas**

LEARNING OBJECTIVES

- Analyze cause and effect
- Recognize order of adjectives
- Recognize metaphors
- Learn how to structure paragraphs

Building Your Vocabulary

Work in a small group. Look at these phrases and idioms. Discuss their meanings and check with another group if you are uncertain. Use each one in a sentence.

Reading: Identify and interpret figurative language and words with multiple meanings

carry out a tradition

to this day

straight-A student

clear your throat

spring fever

time-consuming job

Reading Strategy

Identify cause and effect   Every event, whether it occurs in a story or the real world, has a cause. On the other hand, every cause can result in an important effect. Go over the points below to identify causes and effects.

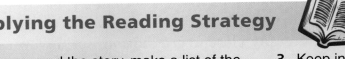

Applying the Reading Strategy

1. As you read the story, make a list of the important events that take place.

2. Find a cause for each important event on your list. Make a Cause and Effect chart. Write causes on the left and effects on the right. Try to find the cause, or reason, that each story event occurred.

3. Keep in mind that a single cause can result in more than one effect. A single effect can also have more than one cause. Chains of cause and effect can occur when a cause results in an effect—and that effect, in turn, becomes the cause of a new effect.

4. Use your Cause and Effect chart to analyze and better understand the story.

The Scholarship Jacket   173

The Scholarship Jacket

a story by Marta Salinas

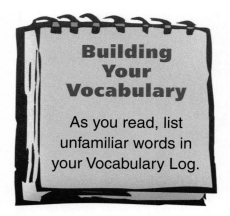

Building Your Vocabulary

As you read, list unfamiliar words in your Vocabulary Log.

As You Read

1. What school tradition is carried out at the eighth grade graduation?

2. Why does the author live with her grandparents? Look for the cause.

3. Why does she expect to win the jacket?

4. Find the reasons why the author and her sister can not participate in sports.

The small Texas school that I attended carried out a tradition every year during the eighth grade graduation; a beautiful gold and green jacket, the school colors, was awarded to the class valedictorian, the student who had maintained the highest grades for eight years. The scholarship jacket had a big gold *S* on the left front side and the winner's name was written in gold letters on the pocket.

My oldest sister Rosie had won the jacket a few years back and I fully expected to win also. I was fourteen and in the eighth grade. I had been a straight A student since the first grade, and the last year I had looked forward to owning that jacket. My father was a farm laborer who couldn't earn enough money to feed eight children, so when I was six I was given to my grandparents to raise. We couldn't participate in sports at school because there were registration fees, uniform costs, and trips out of town; so even though we were quite agile and athletic, there would never be a sports school jacket for us. This one, the scholarship jacket, was our only chance.

In May, close to graduation, spring fever struck, and no one paid any attention in class; instead we stared out the windows and at each other, wanting to speed up the last few weeks of school. I despaired every time I looked in the mirror. Pencil thin, not a curve anywhere, I was called "Beanpole" and "String Bean" and I knew that's what I looked like. A flat chest, no hips, and a brain, that's what I had. That really isn't much for a fourteen-year-old to work

agile: quick and well-coordinated

Reading: Recognize cause-and-effect relationships in a text

with, I thought, as I absentmindedly wandered from my history class to the gym. Another hour of sweating in basketball and displaying my toothpick legs was coming up. Then I remembered my P.E. shorts were still in a bag under my desk where I'd forgotten them. I had to walk all the way back and get them. Coach Thompson was a real bear if anyone wasn't dressed for P.E. She had said I was a good forward and once she even tried to talk Grandma into letting me join the team. Grandma, of course, said no.

I was almost back at my classroom's door when I heard angry voices and arguing. I stopped. I didn't mean to eavesdrop; I just hesitated, not knowing what to do. I needed those shorts and I was going to be late, but I didn't want to interrupt an argument between my teachers. I recognized the voices: Mr. Schmidt, my history teacher, and Mr. Boone, my math teacher. They seemed to be arguing about me. I couldn't believe it. I still remember the shock that rooted me flat against the wall as if I were trying to blend in with the graffiti written there.

"I refuse to do it! I don't care who her father is, her grades don't even begin to compare to Martha's. I won't lie or falsify records. Martha has a straight A plus average and you know it." That was Mr. Schmidt and he sounded very angry. Mr. Boone's voice sounded calm and quiet.

"Look, Joann's father is not only on the Board, he owns the only store in town; we could say it was a close tie and—"

P.E.: physical education
eavesdrop: listen in secret
Martha: the English version of her Spanish name, Marta

Reading: Recognize cause-and-effect relationships in a text

The pounding in my ears drowned out the rest of the words, only a word here and there filtered through. ". . . Martha is Mexican. . . . resign. . . . won't do it. . . ." Mr. Schmidt came rushing out, and luckily for me went down the opposite way toward the auditorium, so he didn't see me. Shaking, I waited a few minutes and then went in and grabbed my bag and fled from the room. Mr. Boone looked up when I came in but didn't say anything. To this day I don't remember if I got in trouble in P.E. for being late or how I made it through the rest of the afternoon. I went home very sad and cried into my pillow that night so Grandmother wouldn't hear me. It seemed a cruel <mark>coincidence</mark> that I had overhead that conversation.

The next day when the principal called me into his office, I knew what it would be about. He looked uncomfortable and unhappy. I decided I wasn't going to make it any easier for him so I looked him straight in the eye. He looked away and fidgeted with the papers on his desk.

"Martha," he said, "there's been a change in policy this year regarding the scholarship jacket. As you know, it has always been free." He cleared his throat and continued. "This year the Board decided to charge fifteen dollars—which still won't cover the complete cost of the jacket."

I stared at him in shock and a small sound of dismay escaped my throat. I hadn't expected this. He still avoided looking in my eyes.

"So if you are unable to pay the fifteen dollars for the jacket, it will be given to the next one in line."

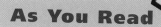

As You Read

1. How does the principal act in front of Marta?

2. How much will the school charge for the jacket?

coincidence: something that happens at the same time as something else

Reading: Recognize cause-and-effect relationships in a text

Standing with all the dignity I could muster, I said, "I'll speak to my grandfather about it, sir, and let you know tomorrow." I cried on the walk home from the bus stop. The dirt road was a quarter of a mile from the highway, so by the time I got home, my eyes were red and puffy.

"Where's Grandpa?" I asked Grandma, looking down at the floor so she wouldn't ask me why I'd been crying. She was sewing on a quilt and didn't look up.

"I think he's out back working in the bean field."

I went outside and looked out at the fields. There he was. I could see him walking between the rows, his body bent over the little plants, hoe in hand. I walked slowly out to him, trying to think how I could best ask him for the money. There was a cool breeze blowing and a sweet smell of mesquite in the air, but I didn't appreciate it. I kicked at a dirt clod. I wanted that jacket so much. It was more than just being a valedictorian and giving a little thank you speech for the jacket on graduation night. It represented eight years of hard work and expectation. I knew I had to be honest with Grandpa; it was my only chance. He saw me and looked up.

He waited for me to speak. I cleared my throat nervously and clasped my hands behind my back so he wouldn't see them shaking. "Grandpa, I have a big favor to ask you," I said in Spanish, the only language he knew. He still waited silently. I tried

muster: gather or assemble
mesquite: a spiny tree that commonly grows in Texas

Reading: Recognize cause-and-effect relationships in a text

again. "Grandpa, this year the principal said the scholarship jacket is not going to be free. It's going to cost fifteen dollars and I have to take the money in tomorrow, otherwise it'll be given to someone else." The last words came out in an eager rush. Grandpa straightened up tiredly and leaned his chin on the hoe handle. He looked out over the field that was filled with the tiny green bean plants. I waited, desperately hoping he'd say I could have the money.

Reading: Recognize cause-and-effect relationships in a text

He turned to me and asked quietly, "What does a scholarship jacket mean?"

I answered quickly; maybe there was a chance. "It means you've earned it by having the highest grades for eight years and that's why they're giving it to you." Too late I realized the significance of my words. Grandpa knew that I understood it was not a matter of money. It wasn't that. He went back to hoeing the weeds that sprang up between the delicate little bean plants. It was a time-consuming job; sometimes the small shoots were right next to each other. Finally he spoke again.

"Then if you pay for it, Marta, it's not a scholarship jacket, is it? Tell your principal I will not pay the fifteen dollars."

As You Read

1. How much does Marta tell her grandpa that the scholarship jacket cost?

2. Why will her grandfather not pay for the scholarship jacket?

shoots: the first sprouts of a growing plant

Reading: Recognize cause-and-effect relationships in a text

I walked back to the house and locked myself in the bathroom for a long time. I was angry with Grandfather even though I knew he was right, and I was angry with the Board, whoever they were. Why did they have to change the rules just when it was my turn to win the jacket?

It was a very sad and withdrawn girl who dragged into the principal's office the next day. This time he did look me in the eyes.

"What did your grandfather say?"

I sat very straight in my chair.

"He said to tell you he won't pay the fifteen dollars."

The principal muttered something I couldn't understand under his breath, and walked over to the window. He stood looking out at something outside. He looked bigger than usual when he stood up; he was a tall gaunt man with gray hair, and I watched the back of his head while I waited for him to speak.

"Why?" he finally asked. "Your grandfather has the money. Doesn't he own a small bean farm?"

I looked at him, forcing my eyes to stay dry. "He said if I had to pay for it, then it wouldn't be a scholarship jacket," I said and stood up to leave. "I guess you'll just have to give it to Joann." I hadn't meant to say that; it had just slipped out. I was almost to the door when he stopped me.

"Martha—wait."

I turned and looked at him, waiting. What did he want now? I could feel my heart pounding.

gaunt: thin

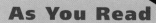

As You Read

1. What does the principal look like?

2. What kind of farm does the grandfather own?

Reading: Recognize cause-and-effect relationships in a text

Something bitter and vile tasting was coming up in my mouth; I was afraid I was going to be sick. I didn't need any sympathy speeches. He sighed loudly and went back to his big desk. He looked at me, biting his lip, as if thinking.

"Okay. We'll make an exception in your case. I'll tell the Board, you'll get your jacket."

I could hardly believe it. I spoke in a trembling rush. "Oh, thank you, sir!" Suddenly I felt great. I didn't know about adrenaline in those days, but I knew something was pumping through me, making

adrenaline: a hormone that increases blood pressure

Reading: Recognize cause-and-effect relationships in a text

me feel as tall as the sky. I wanted to yell, jump, run the mile, do something. I ran out so I could cry in the hall where there was no one to see me. At the end of the day, Mr. Schmidt winked at me and said, "I hear you're getting a scholarship jacket this year."

His face looked as happy and innocent as a baby's, but I knew better. Without answering I gave him a quick hug and ran to the bus. I cried on the walk home again, but this time because I was so happy. I couldn't wait to tell Grandpa and ran straight to the field. I joined him in the row where he was working and without saying anything I crouched down and started pulling up the weeds with my hands. Grandpa worked alongside me for a few minutes, but he didn't ask what had happened. After I had a little pile of weeds between the rows, I stood up and faced him.

Reading: Recognize cause-and-effect relationships in a text

"The principal said he's making an exception for me, Grandpa, and I'm getting the jacket after all. That's after I told him what you said."

Grandpa didn't say anything, he just gave me a pat on the shoulder and a smile. He pulled out the crumpled red handkerchief that he always carried in his back pocket and wiped the sweat off his forehead.

"Better go see if your grandmother needs any help with supper."

I gave him a big grin. He didn't fool me. I skipped and ran back to the house whistling some silly tune.

As You Read

1. What does Mr. Schmidt say to Marta?
2. What is Grandpa's response to Marta's news?

About the Author

Marta Salinas

A Mexican American living in California, Marta Salinas writes about growing up as a Chicana. The reading "The Scholarship Jacket" appears in a collection of readings called *Nosotras: Latina Literature Today*. The author's stories have also been published in the *Los Angeles Herald Examiner* and in *California Living*.

Reading: Recognize cause-and-effect relationships in a text

After You Read

Retell It!

With a partner, compare your lists of causes and effects and the notes you took as you read the reading. Divide the reading in half so that each of you has an opportunity to speak. Retell the story using your notes and lists of causes and effects. Only give the details that are important for moving the story from event to event. Use words such as **as, so, why,** and **because**.

Think, Discuss, Write

Work in small groups. Discuss these questions and write down your answers on a separate sheet of paper.

1. **Recall details**   Who is Joann? Why might she get the scholarship jacket?

2. **Recall details**   How does Marta's grandfather react when she tells him she must pay for the jacket?

3. **Cause and effect**   What happens to make the principal change his mind about giving the jacket to Marta? Why do you think he changes his mind?

4. **Compare and contrast**   How are Mr. Boone and Mr. Schmidt different? Which of these men is more admirable? Why?

5. **Predict**   What do you think would have happened if Marta had not overheard the argument between Mr. Boone and Mr. Schmidt?

6. **Point of view**   Who is the narrator in this reading? How does this help you understand Marta's thoughts and feelings?

Literary response: Identify events that advance the plot and determine how each event explains or foreshadows actions

7. **Make inferences**   How do you think Joann would feel if Marta told her how she eventually got the jacket?

What's Your Opinion?

Work with a partner. Suppose that one of you is Mr. Boone and one is Mr. Schmidt. Have a discussion about who should get the jacket, Marta or Joann. Try to be as convincing as you can.

Launch into Grammar

Order of adjectives   When more than one adjective is used to describe a noun, a special order is often used. The adjective that states a person's *opinion* comes first, followed by *size, age, color, nationality* (Korean, Dutch), and *material* (glass, plastic).

(opinion)   (age)   (color)

Example: the beautiful, brand-new, gold and green jacket

With a partner, copy the following phrases on a sheet of paper. Insert the adjectives in parentheses that are in the correct order.

1. the _____ school (Texas, small **or** small, Texas)

2. the _____ S on the jacket (big, gold **or** gold, big)

3. the _____ girl (talented, fourteen-year-old, Mexican **or** fourteen-year-old, Mexican, talented)

4. the _____ bean plants (new, green **or** green, new)

Written conventions: Identify and use adjectives correctly in writing and speaking

5. the _____ tradition (Spanish, important, old **or** important, old, Spanish)

 For more practice with adjectives, complete page 107 of the Student Workbook.

Launch into Word Analysis

Metaphors   One way authors can describe someone or something more clearly is to use a metaphor. A metaphor compares two unlike things without the use of the words *like* or *as*. Here is an example:

> **Example:** Coach Thompson <u>was a real bear</u> if anyone wasn't dressed for P.E.

Work in a small group. Create a metaphor that describes Marta, Mr. Schmidt, Grandpa, and the principal. Share your metaphors with the class.

> **Extend:** Watch for metaphors in your textbooks and outside reading.

 For more practice with metaphors, complete page 108 of the Student Workbook.

Launch into Writing

Structure paragraphs   In this story, the author provides information and **supporting details** to better communicate the storyline. Works of nonfiction also provide information and details. Paragraphs of a nonfiction work often contain a topic or introductory

A grizzly bear.

Reading: Understand and explain the figurative and metaphorical use of words in context

sentence that explains what the paragraph is about and continue with details that relate to the topic sentence.

Practice structuring paragraphs by writing a response to the situation described in "The Scholarship Jacket." Suppose you were Marta and you wanted to write a letter to the school about next year's scholarship jacket. Should the winner have to pay for the jacket?

Here is an example:

Michigan State Spartans head coach Tom Izzo.

> I am writing to inform you that I don't think the winner of the scholarship jacket should need to pay for the jacket. If the jacket winner <u>earns</u> the jacket, then he or she shouldn't need to pay for it. If you are going to <u>buy</u> a jacket, then why make a big fuss about <u>winning</u> it? Just go to the store and buy a jacket on your own!

For more practice with structuring paragraphs, complete pages 110–111 of the Student Workbook.

Writing: Create a single paragraph: Develop a topic sentence, and include simple supporting facts and details

15

Racing a Champion

an essay by
Michael Baughman

Background

Have you ever wondered how someone becomes a successful entertainer, artist, or sports star? How much is talent and how much is effort and hard work? The main character in this story raced with a champion and then asked how he had trained to become such a great swimmer. See if you can predict his answer.

LEARNING OBJECTIVES

- Trace an author's perspective
- Use commas with coordinating conjunctions
- Use descriptive language
- Research information

Building Your Vocabulary

1. With a partner, read these words and phrases from "Racing a Champion." Discuss the meanings of these words, which are all related to sports and athletic events. On a separate sheet of paper, write the meanings of the ones you know. Use a dictionary to find the meanings of the others.

swim against me	try out	
compete	dead even	
race	hold this pace	
impressive pace	strokes	
confident	just about even	
strong lead	gold medals	

2. On a separate sheet of paper, use each word or phrase in a sentence of your own. Share your sentences with your partner.

Reading Strategy

Trace the author's perspective Authors approach their subjects from a variety of different **perspectives**, or points of view. When you read, keep a close eye on the author's perspective and how it changes or develops.

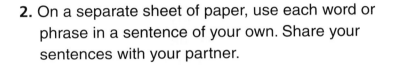

Applying the Reading Strategy

1. Read the beginning of the selection. How much does the author seem to know about the situation he or she is writing about?

2. As the reading moves forward, look for changes in the author's attitude or point of view.

3. In what ways has the author's attitude shifted by the end of the story? What ideas and events caused this shift to occur?

4. After you finish the selection, go back and trace how the author's viewpoint changed over the entire story.

Reading: Use knowledge of the author's purpose to comprehend informational text

Racing a Champion

an essay by Michael Baughman

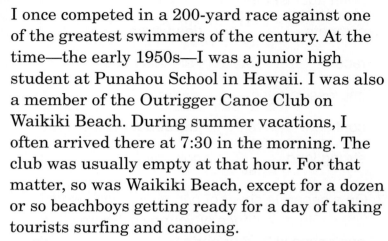

I once competed in a 200-yard race against one of the greatest swimmers of the century. At the time—the early 1950s—I was a junior high student at Punahou School in Hawaii. I was also a member of the Outrigger Canoe Club on Waikiki Beach. During summer vacations, I often arrived there at 7:30 in the morning. The club was usually empty at that hour. For that matter, so was Waikiki Beach, except for a dozen or so beachboys getting ready for a day of taking tourists surfing and canoeing.

There was one other club member who would turn up early on summer mornings, though. He was a tall, handsome, silver-haired Hawaiian. I could tell that he didn't spend a lot of time at the beach because his face was a darker brown than his body. Occasionally I saw him swimming with a slow, graceful stroke that carried him effortlessly along at an impressive pace to the beach wall and back again.

One morning when I'd arrived at the club earlier than usual, I was on the beach loading a two-person canoe for a day of spearing fish. He walked past me on his way to the water. Then he stopped.

"Where do you spear?" he asked.

"Usually by the old sunken barge, out past Baby Surf."

"Do you surf, too?" he asked.

"Sure!" I replied.

"How about swimming?"

"I'm a pretty good swimmer," I said.

As You Read

1. What is the setting of this reading? What does the word *once* tell you about when the reading takes place?

2. Who are the characters in the reading?

3. Describe the Hawaiian man. Do you think he is young? Why or why not?

stroke: a movement of the body in swimming

Reading: Use knowledge of the author's purpose to comprehend informational text

"You probably go to Punahou School, right?"

"Right," I answered.

"You going to try out for their swim team?"

"I already play football and basketball and run track," I said. "You're pretty fast. I'll bet you were on a swim team."

"I was once, a long time ago," he told me. "How would you like to swim against me? Just for fun, I mean."

"Now? Against you?"

"Sure. Just for fun. Down to the beach wall and back." He pointed in that direction. "It's just about 200 yards." He was smiling at me.

"Okay," I said.

We waded into the warm water, out through the gentle waves to a depth of about four or five feet. He smiled again, then said, "Let's go," and started swimming.

Teenagers are often very competitive, and I was no different. Though I was confident of winning, I started to sprint as fast as I could go. I thought I'd build a strong lead at the first 50 yards. But after those 50 yards, we were even. He won't be able to hold this pace for long, I told myself.

When we reached the beach wall, we were still dead even. I was already about three-quarters exhausted. My arms felt heavy. My shoulders started to burn. As we started back, he smiled at me.

"What's going on here?" I thought. "He doesn't look tired at all. He must be faking. He's got to be worse off than I am."

I was able to hold my pace for another 40 or 50 yards, at which point we were still swimming side

sprint: swim quickly

Reading: Use knowledge of the author's purpose to comprehend informational text

by side. By now, though, I was taking two strokes to my opponent's one. My legs were in knots. My arms and shoulders were numb, and my head was spinning. I wanted very badly to quit and walk the rest of the way.

I struggled and made it, fighting the water, which felt like warm molasses.

"Just about even," he said, when we finally stopped in front of the club.

I was panting for breath. "Guess so," I said, trying not to show it.

"Thanks for the swim," he added.

"Sure."

"You're pretty good all right. But you might as well stay with football, basketball, and track," he told me.

"Well . . . sure," I said.

"See you later."

He walked out of the water and up the beach. I stayed where I was, recovering.

Ten minutes later my friend, Sammy Kauua, arrived. I told him some of what had happened.

"See that old guy standing by the canoe?" I said.

"He's a pretty good swimmer. I swam down to the beach wall and back with him. Who is he, anyway?"

Sammy laughed. "Are you kidding? Where have you been all your life? Wake up! That's Duke Kahanamoku. He won gold medals at the Olympics. I guess he's pretty good for sure!"

That night I looked him up in an almanac. Duke Kahanamoku had won a gold and a silver

almanac: a book of records

Reading: Use knowledge of the author's purpose to comprehend informational text

medal in 1912 and two golds in 1920. He had also won a silver in 1924. He was past 60 when I "raced" against him.

Several days later when I saw Kahanamoku on the beach, I talked to him about his swimming career. What I really wanted to know was how an athlete could become good enough to win in the Olympics.

"How hard did you have to train?" I asked him. "I mean, how many miles a day did you have to swim?"

"Oh, I trained," he said. "But not hard, really. I did most of my swimming at the beach. I swam after my surfboard when a wave washed it in. I swam because I liked it. It was always fun, and I was pretty good at it. We trained all right, but mostly we just swam. It was natural. I always enjoyed doing it."

I was disappointed at the time because there was no easy answer there, no secret formula for success as an athlete. Thinking back on it now, though, I find the answer he gave me very appealing.

appealing: attractive or encouraging

As You Read

1. How many medals did Duke Kahanamoku win?

2. Where did Kahanamoku spend most of his time training for the Olympics?

About the Author

Michael Baughman

Michael Baughman is an Emeritus Professor at Southern Oregon University in Ashland, Oregon. He has written books on Native American life and on outdoor recreation in the American West.

Reading: Use knowledge of the author's purpose to comprehend informational text

Hawaiian surfer Rochelle Ballard.

Retell It!

With a partner, talk about the race and Duke Kahanamoku. One of you will be the narrator and the other will be Sammy Kauua. Ask each other questions so that you are able to mention the main events of the reading. Use expressive words, gestures, and correct pronunciation.

Think, Discuss, Write

Work in small groups. Discuss the following questions and write down your answers on a separate sheet of paper.

1. **Recall details**   At what point in the story do you know all of the details about the characters? How do you know?

2. **Recall details**   How does the narrator know that the man does not spend much time at the beach?

3. **Make inferences**   Why do you think Sammy laughs when the boy asks who Duke is?

4. **Compare and contrast**   What other sports does the boy play? How does swimming differ from these sports?

5. **Cause and effect**   What is Duke's answer for training? Do you think it will change the way the boy plays sports?

6. **Point of view**   From what point of view is the reading written? How do you know this?

7. **Title**   What do you think the title of the reading would be if it were told from Duke Kahanamoku's point of view? Why?

Reading: Retell the central ideas of expository or narrative passages

What's Your Opinion?

Work in small groups. Discuss the two main characters in the reading. On a separate sheet of paper, write down the things you know about their personalities. Put a + next to the characteristics that you think are positive and a − next to the ones that are negative. Share your opinions with another group.

Professional surfer John Shimooka.

Launch into Grammar

Commas with coordinating conjunctions   When words or word groups have equal importance in a sentence, they are joined by a **coordinating conjunction—and, but, or,** or **so**. When coordinating conjunctions join two clauses, they use a comma.

> **Examples:** **No comma**: I already play football **and** basketball.
> **No comma**: I wanted very badly to quit **and** walk the rest of the way.
> **Comma**: Teenagers are often very competitive, **and** I was no different.

Copy each sentence onto a sheet of paper. Place a comma into the correct place in the sentence if it is needed.

1. He walked out of the water and up the beach.

2. We trained all right but mostly we just swam.

3. I struggled and made it.

Written conventions: Identify and use coordinating conjunctions in writing

4. I wanted to win so I started to sprint right away.

5. My arms were numb and my head was spinning.

 For more practice using commas with coordinating conjunctions, complete page 115 of the Student Workbook.

Launch into Word Analysis

Use descriptive language One of an author's most important goals is to help the reader see a scene as the author imagines it. Descriptive words help readers see, feel, smell, touch, and taste what is being described.

> **Example:** His face was a darker brown than the rest of his body.

With a partner, write the following sentences on a separate sheet of paper. Think of a descriptive word that can fit into each space. After you are finished, compare the words you wrote to the actual words in the story.

1. Occasionally I saw him swimming with a _____ stroke.

2. My arms and shoulders were _____, and my head was _____.

3. I struggled and made it, fighting the water, which felt like _____.

4. I was _____ for breath.

 For more practice using descriptive language, complete page 116 of the Student Workbook.

Writing: Use descriptive words when writing

Launch into Writing

Georgia High School Association relay competition.

Research information   When you want to find out more about a topic, you need to do research. Research is usually a three-step process. First, you must find a topic. Second, you need to find sources. Finally, you need to take notes on the information your sources provide.

Select a sport or outdoor activity that you would like to learn more about, such as swimming, biking, or football. Then locate information sources for this topic. Take notes on notecards like the one shown below.

Topic: Biking
Source: Magazine article: "Finding the Best Bike for You," by Clive Roper, in American Leisure, August 2001.
Notes: 1. Kind of biking: (a) racing, (b) mountain biking, (c) touring, (d) dirt biking BMX. 2. Money: how much can you spend? 3. Type: (a) "Pro," (b) Experienced, (c) Beginner. 4. Landscape: (a) city/town, (b) country, (c) flat, (d) hills.

For more practice researching information, complete pages 118–119 of the Student Workbook.

Writing: Understand the organization of newspapers and periodicals and how to use those print materials

16

Before You Read

Background

Have you ever set a big goal for yourself? Did someone else inspire you to do it? Identifying with a person you have something in common with can motivate you to succeed. As you read the poem "Marathon," think about a time when an athlete, a member of your family, a scholar, or someone else inspired you.

marathon

**a poem by
Janet S. Wong**

LEARNING OBJECTIVES

- Identify themes across sources
- Change passive voice to active voice
- Identify connotations and denotations
- Learn to make bibliographies

Building Your Vocabulary

1. Work with a partner. A **marathon** is a kind of race. Look at the list of words. How many of them do you know? They all have to do with walking and running. Fill out a chart like the one on page 199 on a separate sheet of paper, separating the words into the two categories.

walk	promenade
run	sprint
stroll	amble
saunter	hasten

Reading: Classify grade-appropriate categories of words

Walking	Running
Stroll	*Sprint*

2. Discuss with a partner. Which word in your chart describes the slowest action? Which describes the fastest?

Reading Strategy

Identify themes across sources   Every poem is unique. But when you look more deeply into a poem you begin to see ideas, or themes, that repeat themselves. Two poems that seem very different may both be about the same thing. When you read a poem, look for themes that you have seen in other poems or other types of literature.

Applying the Reading Strategy

1. Read the poem carefully and identify its theme. Common themes include truth, family, friendship, happiness, competition, and beauty.

2. Once the theme is identified, think back to other sources you are familiar with that have a similar theme, such as a poem, a play, a movie, or a story.

3. Compare the themes of the different sources. How were they the same? How were they different?

Reading: Connect and clarify main ideas by identifying their relationships to other sources

marathon

a poem by Janet S. Wong

I hope the Chinese
wins the race.

I see myself
in her face.

Does she see me
in this crowd?

Chinese: the Chinese runner

Reading: Connect and clarify main ideas by identifying their relationships to other sources

Does she hear me
cheering loud?

When I am grown
but not too old—

I'll run this race.
And win the gold.

About the Author

Janet S. Wong

Janet S. Wong was born in Los Angeles, California. Her father was a Chinese immigrant and her mother was from Korea. She writes poems that deal with family and heritage and celebrate her multicultural background. She has won awards for her book *A Suitcase of Seaweed and Other Poems,* and *Good Luck Gold.*

Reading: Connect and clarify main ideas by identifying their relationships to other sources

After You Read

Retell It!

With a partner, retell the story to each other in prose. Change the point of view from first person to third person, so you will be speaking *about* the people in the poem.

Think, Discuss, Write

Work in small groups. Discuss the following questions and write your answers on a separate sheet of paper.

1. **Scan poetry**   What is the rhyme pattern in this poem?

2. **Theme**   Which words or phrases are repeated in the poem?

3. **Structure**   How is the form of the poem important?

4. **Make inferences**   What ethnicity is the runner? Why is this important to the poet?

5. **Compare and contrast**   What does this poem have in common with "Racing a Champion"? How are they different?

6. **Idiom**   What do you think the sentence "I see myself in her face" means?

7. **Point of view**   From whose point of view is this poem written? How is this important?

What's Your Opinion?

With a partner, discuss the four selections you have read in this unit about goals. Think about other

Reading: Respond to *who, what, when, where,* and *how* questions poems, stories, and nonfiction articles you have read. On a separate sheet of paper, fill in a chart like the one below and give a grade to each of the characteristics of each type of literature.

	Characteristics				
	Interesting Language	Informative	Fun to Read	Easy to Understand	Made Me Think
Poetry	a	B	B	B	a
Stories					
Nonfiction					

Launch into Grammar

Active and passive voice   The **active** voice uses action verbs to identify exactly what takes place. The **passive** voice is less clear about who does the action in a sentence.

Examples: I **run** this race.
The verb *run* is **active**. The sentence tells exactly who does the action.

This race was **run**.
The verb is **passive**. The sentence doesn't tell who did the action.

The active voice is generally stronger and more direct than the passive voice. When a writer doesn't want to identify someone directly, he or she may use the passive voice.

With a partner, search through the poem and find two active voice sentences. Rewrite those sentences on a

Written conventions: Identify and use verb tenses properly in writing and speaking

separate sheet of paper and change the active voice to the passive voice.

For more practice with active and passive voice, complete page 123 of the Student Workbook.

Launch into Word Analysis

Connotation and denotation A word's **denotation** is its dictionary definition. Some words have **connotations** as well as denotations. The connotation of a word includes feelings, memories, and thoughts that may be connected to the word. For example, **house** usually refers to a building. A **home**, on the other hand, has the connotation of being a warm, safe, and comfortable place.

On a sheet of paper, copy the chart below. Each word on the chart comes from the poem "Marathon." Circle each choice to show the correct denotation and connotation for each word.

Word	Denotation		Connotation	
gold	yellow metal	red color	victory success	shame loss
crowd	large thing	group of people	not enough	too many
grown	young	an adult	weak and old	wise, strong
old	large	not young	fast	feeble

For more practice with connotation and denotation, complete page 124 of the Student Workbook.

Reading: Understand and explain the figurative and metaphorical use of words in context

Launch into Writing

Make bibliographies   When you use sources in your writing, you should include a bibliography to identify each source that you used. A **bibliography** is a list of books (and sometimes other sources) that the reader can use to find out more about a topic. Here is a bibliography that might be used for the poem "Marathon."

Galloway, Jeff, *Marathon!* Phidippides Books, 2000

Martin, David E., and Gynn, Roger, *The Olympic Marathon.* Human Kinetics, 2000

Wong, Janet, and Wallace, John, *Grump.* Margaret McElderry, 2001

Wong, Janet, *A Suitcase of Seaweed.* Simon and Schuster, 1996

   Get a list of sources for your own bibliography. With a partner, choose a topic for your sources, such as marathon running, famous marathon champions, or history of the marathon. On a sheet of paper, write your sources in the form shown above. Use the library or the Internet to find sources.

 For more practice writing bibliographies, complete pages 126–127 of the Student Workbook.

Writing: Quote or paraphrase information sources, citing them appropriately

Deliver a Research Report

Work in small groups to prepare a research report on the subject of Goals. As a group, research the topic, make notes, and prepare visual aids. Present your research to the class.

Step One:
Plan Your Research Report

1. As a group, brainstorm a list of topics. Vote for the one you will research.

2. Break the topic up into subtopics or categories. Then, divide up and research those subtopics, taking notes on notecards just as you would for a research report.

3. Share the information that you have found. As a group, decide whether any of this information is unnecessary. Do not include unnecessary information in the report.

4. Identify and use visual aids, such as diagrams, drawings, or video segments, that help your audience better understand your report.

5. Compile the notes to prepare your group research report. Decide who will present each subtopic. Each person should take notes on notecards to identify important points that they will present. Taking notes will help you to recall important information. Since your research will be presented orally in class, you do not need to write out every word that you will say.

Step Two:
Practice Your Research Report

Now practice presenting your report. Record a practice presentation and listen to the recording. Take notes about how you can improve it. Discuss the best features of the presentation.

Step Three:
Present Your Research Report

Once you have practiced your research report, polish your work and present it to the class.

Step Four:
Evaluate Your Research Report

After your presentation, invite classmates to ask questions or provide comments. Did your classmates feel that you included all the important points? Did they like your delivery?

Speaking: Deliver research presentations: Pose relevant questions, convey clear perspectives, and include evidence from research

Record Your Research Report

Add a tape of your presentation to the classroom listening lab. Listen to your own and others' tapes. Bring a tape to share with family members.

Speaking Checklist

✔ I used an appropriate tone of voice.

✔ I spoke slowly enough to be clear.

✔ I used appropriate gestures. I did not do anything that would distract my audience.

✔ I made eye contact with the audience. I looked at each person while speaking.

Speaking: Deliver research presentations: Pose relevant questions, convey clear perspectives, and include evidence from research

Write a Research Report

Think about a hobby or other subject that you find interesting. Write a research report that tells about this particular subject. Include factual information in order to support your points.

Here is an example:

> *Ants*
>
> Ants are small insects that some people find bothersome. However, they are very interesting creatures. They make their own homes, work hard, and are helpful to nature and humans.
>
> An ant colony is extremely well-organized. Each ant has a special job in the colony. Each colony has one queen whose main job is to lay eggs.

1. Pre-write

Before you begin researching your topic, plan the structure of your report. How many paragraphs will you have? How many subtopics do you need to support your opening paragraph? Organize the subtopics, facts, and details for your report by taking notes on cards and writing an outline.

2. Draft

Follow these steps to organize your research report:

A. Introduce the topic. Use the opening paragraph to introduce the main topic.

B. Organize the subtopics. Determine your subtopics and create one paragraph about each.

C. Supply supporting facts. Add facts and details to support each subtopic.

D. Conclude with a summary. Summarize your main topic and subtopics in the last paragraph.

E. Write a bibliography that lists all the sources that you referred to when researching and writing your report.

Writing: Write research reports: Pose relevant questions, support the main idea, and include a bibliography

3. Revise

Reread your draft and ask yourself these questions:

- Have I introduced my topic effectively?
- Does the order of my subtopics make sense?
- Do I need to add more facts or details about any of the subtopics?
- Have I summarized my main topic and subtopics in the conclusion?

Consider your answers to these questions as you revise your research report. Ask a classmate to answer these same questions about your report. Make any additional changes based on your classmate's feedback.

4. Edit and Proofread

Proofread your revised report. Check sentence punctuation, capitalization, and spelling. Look in the dictionary to verify spelling.

5. Publish

Create a multimedia presentation, using drawings, diagrams, video, slides or music to support your report. As you present your report to the class, use appropriate gestures and body language during the presentation.

Goals Collage

Project Goal

Create a puzzle that shows what you would like to achieve as you grow older: things you would like to learn and to do, the job you would like to have, or the place you would like to live.

1. Think about what your goals are. Choose the five goals that are most important to you.

2. For each goal, draw or find a picture that **depicts** that **achievement.** Draw your pictures on a piece of paper, cut photos out of magazines, or find images on the Internet and print them out. For instance, if your goal is to become a veterinarian (animal doctor) someday, you might draw or find a picture of someone caring for a pet.

3. Use your pictures to create a **collage** on a thick sheet of paper. Glue each picture on the paper. Once the glue dries, decorate any blank space with paint or markers.

4. Cut the collage into pieces that are about an inch wide. Make certain you cut with curvy lines and angles, so the pieces take interesting and **unique** (one-of-a-kind) shapes. These are your puzzle pieces.

5. Exchange your puzzle with a partner to piece back together. See if you can tell what each other's goals are.

Words to Know

achievement
collage
unique
depicts

Choose one or more of the following books to write about. Write down in your Reading Log titles of the books you read and your opinion of each one. Ask yourself these questions:

1. What type of goals or dreams have the people in the stories and readings set for themselves?

2. What type of struggles did they face while trying to attain their goals?

3. What type of help and support do they gain on the way? What do they learn from others?

4. What does this book tell you about personal goals and dreams?

Nonfiction

How to Read Faster by Bill Cosby
    The famous actor and comic reveals the secrets to reading quickly and accurately.

Take a Stand! by Daniel Weizmann
    Learn how to run for school office and get involved in your community in this helpful guide.

Fiction

The Laughing Tomato and Other Spring Poems by Francisco Alarcón, illustrated by Maya Gonzalez
    This collection of poems in English and Spanish celebrate everyday achievements and victories.

Reading: Compare and contrast information on the same topic

Credits

ILLUSTRATIONS AND PHOTOGRAPHS

Baughman, Michael: 193; Beebe, Morton/CORBIS: 74; Bettmann/CORBIS: 29; Conger, Dean/CORBIS: 149; CORBIS: 2, 5, 6, 7, 61; de Saint-Exupery, Antoine: 22, 25, 27, 28; Diaz, David: icons; Doss, Laura/CORBIS: 52; Doyle, Rick/CORBIS: 195; Drennan, Rick: 64, 65, 120, 123, 188, 190, 191, 192, 193; EyeWire: 32, 189; 207; Fleming, Kevin/CORBIS: 197; Fogden, Michael & Patricia/CORBIS: 100; Franken, Owen/CORBIS: 47; 103; Franz, D. Robert/CORBIS: 32; Geller, Morissa: 12, 15, 16, 17; Grossman, Myron: 90, 91, 92, 93, 94, 95, 96, 97, 98, 99; Gulin, Darrell/CORBIS: 30; Hayes, Sarah: 139; Heinle & Heinle: 8, 19; Hollingsworth, Jack/CORBIS: 202; Kaehler, Wolfgang/CORBIS: 43; Lang, Otto/CORBIS: 145; Maslen, Barbara: 34, 37, 38, 39, 40, 41, 128, 130, 131, 132, 133, 134, 135, 136, 137, 138; McNamee, Wally/CORBIS: 110; Myers, Jeffrey W./CORBIS: 20; Ott, Kristi: 54, 55, 129, 144, 147, 161, 163, 164, 165, 166, 167; Philbrook, Diana: 198, 200; PhotoDisk: 9, 10, 11, 21, 31, 45, 60, 62, 63, 67, 68, 86, 87, 88, 89, 116, 117, 119, 124, 125, 126, 141, 142, 143, 150, 151, 158, 168, 169, 184, 185, 196, 204, 205; Pierce, L.S.: 76, 78, 79, 80, 81, 82, 83, 85, 172, 175, 177, 178, 180, 181, 182, 183; Pollak, Barbara: 112, 114, 115; Ressmeyer, Roger/CORBIS: 31, 77; Reuters NewMedia Inc./CORBIS: 187, 194; Rothman, Jeffrey L./CORBIS: 42, 44; Rowan, Bob, Progressive Image/CORBIS: 18; Rykoff Collection/CORBIS: 58; Schafer, Kevin/CORBIS: 102; Souders, Paul A./CORBIS: 186; Su, Keren/CORBIS: 33; Turnley, David/CORBIS: 148; Weinberg, Deirdre: 4, 6, 34.

AUTHORS

Unit 1: Friendship

P. 6. "Friendly in a Friendly Way," from *The Collected Poems of Langston Hughes* by Langston Hughes, copyright © 1994 by The Estate of Langston Hughes. Used by permission of Alfred A. Knopf, a division of Random House, Inc.

Pp. 14–17. "Yang's First Friend," from *Yang the Youngest and His Terrible Ear,* copyright © 1992 by Lensey Namioka. Used by permission of Lensey Namioka. All rights are reserved by the author.

Pp. 24–29. "The Fox," excerpts from *The Little Prince* by Antoine de Saint-Exupéry, copyright 1943 and renewed 1971 by Harcourt, Inc., reprinted by permission of the publisher.

Pp. 36–41, "Greg and Willie," from *Helping Hands* by Suzanne Haldane, copyright © 1991 by Suzanne Haldane. Used by permission of Dutton Children's Books, an imprint of Penguin Putnam Books for Young Readers, a division of Penguin Putnam, Inc.,

Unit 2: Courage

Pp. 56–59. From *The Last Princess* by Fay Grissom Stanley, copyright © 1994 by Fay Grissom Stanley. Used by permission of HarperCollins Publishers, Inc.

Pp. 66–71. "Emma Garcia: Community Organizer at Age 16," from *Extraordinary Young People* by Marlene Targ Brill, copyright © 1996 by Marlene Targ Brill, used with permission of Children's Press, Inc., a division of Grolier Publishing Co.

Pp. 78–85. Reprinted with permission of Simon & Schuster Books for Young Readers, an imprint of Simon & Schuster Children's Publishing Division from *Call It Courage* by Armstrong Sperry, copyright © 1940 by Simon & Schuster, Inc., copyright renewed 1968 by Armstrong Sperry.

Pp. 92–98. From *She's Wearing a Dead Bird on Her Head!* by Kathryn Lasky; illustrated by David Catrow. Text © 1995 by Kathryn Lasky. Reprinted by permission of Hyperion Books for Children.

Unit 3: Conflict

P. 114. "Class Bully," copyright © 1999 by Nikki Grimes, from *My Man Blue* by Nikki Grimes, illustrated by Jerome Lagarrigue. Used by permission of Dial Books for Young Readers, an imprint of Penguin Putnam Books for Young Readers, a division of Penguin Putnam, Inc.

Pp. 122–123. "Argument Sticks," from *Peace Tales: World Folktales to Talk About* by Margaret Read MacDonald, copyright © 1992 by Margaret Read MacDonald, used with permission of The Shoe String Press.

Pp. 130–139. From *Robin Hood,* retold by Sarah Hayes, text copyright © 1989 by Sarah Hayes, used with permission of Henry Holt and Company, Inc.

Pp. 146–147. From *Zlata's Diary,* by Zlata Filipović, copyright © 1994 Éditions Robert Laffont/Fixot. Used by permission of Viking Penguin, a division of Penguin Putnam, Inc.

Unit 4: Goals

Pp. 162–167. "Setting up an E-Mail Address," from *The Kids' Guide to E-Mail* by Larry P. Stevens and Cara J. Stevens, copyright © 2000 by Larry P. Stevens and Cara J. Stevens, illustrations by Paul Gilligan. Used by permission of The McGraw-Hill Companies. Excerpts from pages 14–26.

Pp. 174–183. From *The Scholarship Jacket,* reprinted with permission with the permission of the publisher, Bilingual Press/Editorial Bilingue, Arizona State University, Tempe, AZ. "The Scholarship Jacket" by Marta Salinas, from *Nosotras: Latina Literature Today,* edited by Maria del Carmen Boza, Beverly Silva, and Carmen Valle. Copyright © 1986 by Marta Salinas.

Pp. 190–193. *Racing a Champion,* reprinted by permission of the author, Michael Baughman.

Pp. 200–201. "Marathon," reprinted with the permission of Margaret K. McElderry Books, an imprint of Simon & Schuster Children's Publishing Division from *A Suitcase of Seaweed and Other Poems* by Janet S. Wong. Copyright © 1996 Janet S. Wong.

Index